SOUL OF THE HURRICANE

SOUL
OF THE
HURRICANE

*THE PERFECT STORM AND
AN ACCIDENTAL SAILOR*

NELSON SIMON

CHICAGO
REVIEW
PRESS

Published by Chicago Review Press Incorporated
814 North Franklin Street
Chicago, Illinois 60610
ISBN 978-1-64160-408-6

Library of Congress Control Number: 2021942197

Interior design: Nord Compo
Map design: Chris Erichsen

Printed in the United States of America
5 4 3 2 1

For Mami and Selim

and

Nick and Kathleen

In memory of

Yvonne Mitcham Ayoroa
1944–2021

Bob Thomason
1927–2020

Thelma Davis
1940–2020

CONTENTS

———

The crew of *Anne Kristine*. From left to right: Jen Irving, Barbara Treyz, Marty Hanks, Joey Gelband, Peter Abelman, John Nuciforo, Nelson Simon, Laingdon Schmitt, Damion Sailors. PHOTO BY MARY ANN BAKER

HURRICANE ALMA

———

Year: 1966
Category: 3
Highest Sustained Wind: 125 mph

MY FIRST HURRICANE was the year I was seven.
My parents had been to Florida the year before with just my brother, Rob, to see relatives visiting from Bolivia, and they wanted to take me because "Miami looked beautiful," as my mother put it. So, the four of us—Mami, Papi, Rob, and I—packed our car and set off from our house in Adelphi, Maryland, made a quick loop halfway around the Beltway, and began the straight shot down I-95, 1,065 miles to Miami Beach.

It must have been a delicate time for our young family, trying, I suppose, to become more of a *family*. My parents had come to this country in 1961, bringing my grandfather to the DC area for treatment at Walter Reed, the military hospital. Papi, trying to establish his own medical residency, was essentially living at Prince George's County Hospital, while my mother cared for her father in the tiny apartment the three of them shared. They had left my brother and me in La Paz with our grandmother, where we lived apart from them for almost a year.

One day our grandmother told us we were going to "Wa-shing-ton," that sing-song place that had become a fairytale kingdom to me, the faraway land where my parents lived. Suddenly, we were on a plane, Rob and I crying the whole way, from La Paz to Miami then on to Washington National Airport. And then we were getting off in a place that was hot and muggy and strange, and nowhere did we see the aunties and uncles, cousins and nannies who populated the world we knew. That was over. I clung to my abuela as these two smiling, vaguely familiar people approached, their arms reaching for me. "When you first saw me, you weren't sure who I was," my mother would later say. "Your abuela was the mother you knew."

I don't believe we planned to stay forever, but time passed, and we just never left. Soon the family pooled together enough money to buy the little house on Kirston Street that would be our home for the next several years. In 1966, still struggling financially but feeling more settled, Mami and Papi must have thought that our first family vacation would be just the thing. As Mami remembered it:

> We just decided to drive to Miami Beach. We didn't know the names of hotels or prices of hotels. We didn't have that much money. I went into this hotel, I asked how much it would cost for us to stay. We were only going to be there a few days, and they gave me a price for a room with a kitchenette that would be sufficient for the four of us, and we could even make breakfast there if we wanted to.

The next day we came downstairs ready for a day at the beach only to find the staff boarding up the hotel windows. A hurricane was coming, they said, and we had to leave. I wasn't sure what a hurricane was, but this didn't seem the right time to ask. The beach was empty, and the police were directing a long line of cars away from the hotel. Our vacation, it seemed, was over. Papi decided we would drive straight home.

We started out. Looking out the back of the car I could see dark, swirly clouds in the distance, and everything around us had a strange, gray tint. The air had that quality it does just before a storm, the feeling that something is about to happen. I later learned this is because of the falling pressure that accompanies a hurricane. Inside the car everything felt . . . right. My father was at the wheel, my mother beside him. Rob and I knelt on the back seat looking back at where we had been, waiting.

When I remember this day, I picture my dear mother, a woman who has lived so much of her life with a heavy heart, for whom happiness has always seemed as far off as heat lightning in the distance. I see her in this moment, a young woman of twenty-six, not so far past her own childhood, alone with her two boys and her husband. Laughing, she seems to be enjoying our unexpected adventure. She is oblivious to the danger. "I had never heard of a hurricane," Mami told me later, "much less seen one. In Bolivia we lived in little towns, with a river or a pond, so we had nothing to compare it to." In my mind she is happy.

Soon the rain began. With every mile we drove, the rain got harder, the skies darker. My father drove slower and slower, until you could have trotted beside us. Rob and I were restless, so Mami entertained us the best way she knew how—by telling us scary stories. Now, every raindrop brought a new monster, every lightning bolt revealed a new menace. Looking back, it does seem an odd way to calm young boys in a potentially dangerous situation, but it worked. Today I love a good fright, and even at that early age I was drawn to these stories, as if by picturing the bad things out there, beyond our windows, we could feel safer somehow.

Eventually, we realized we were the only car on the highway. And then, lights—eerie flashing red and white lights—appeared behind us.

My father pulled over to the shoulder, and the lights followed close behind. After a moment, a state trooper approached my father's window, looking tired, exasperated, and incredulous all at once. "You do realize there's a hurricane headed this way, right?" he said. My father, in his halting English, explained that we did indeed realize this, and that we were trying to make it home to Maryland. "Folks, you need to get off the road. There's a motel six miles ahead. You need to go there and take shelter. Now." We crawled off, all of us feeling a little chastened, and for the first time I could sense something like fear from my parents.

We pulled into the motel and huddled together in our room's one big bed, listening as the winds got louder and the whole place shook through the night. With each thunderclap I held my mother tighter. Eventually I fell asleep and dreamt that I was looking out the motel window. In my dream the hurricane looked a lot like the twister from *The Wizard of Oz*, which I had seen for the first time not long before.

The next morning the skies had calmed and cleared. We learned from the motel receptionist that the storm had made it impossible to go back to Maryland the way we had come, so at breakfast my parents pulled out a map and charted our course home.

We traveled on state highways and county roads, crisscrossing our way north through Georgia, the Carolinas, Virginia. We stopped at gas stations, scenic overlooks, and, at my insistence, every little country cemetery we came upon. I loved cemeteries and found them oddly comforting. In the South they often consisted of small plots connected to a church or belonging to one family. The dates on the headstones were often over a hundred years old, and I was sure to check for families, to see how many generations were laid to rest together. Looking back, it's difficult to fully understand this impulse, one that stayed with me into adulthood. Perhaps I wanted to imagine the lives of people who had been rooted in one place, families who had lived and died and buried their own in one location. I, who had lost my place, my people, and would live forever in a land that would never seem fully my own.

1

WATER

———

"I just didn't want to go."

—Jonny

EVERYTHING STARTED WITH PETER'S CALL. The explorer Norman Baker would be appearing that night—Wednesday, October 23, 1991—at the Museum of Natural History to talk about his experience sailing with legendary adventurer Thor Heyerdahl, and a group of us would be there. I did not know Norman, but my friends did. Our work pal Jonny knew the Bakers well. And Peter had sailed with the family on their ship *Anne Kristine*.

That day, Peter called me up and said, "Hey, Norman is looking for people to sail his ship to Bermuda."

Peter and I had met the year before at Skadden, Arps, Slate, Meagher & Flom LLP (aka Skadden), the corporate law firm where we worked as proofreaders on the graveyard shift. During the day it was everything you would expect a large corporate law firm to be. But the secret was that they paid proofreaders a decent hourly wage, including an extra two dollars for overnight and weekend shifts; so nested within this bulwark of capitalism was a cadre of artists, actors, musicians, and graduate students, and we'd all convinced ourselves that by working at night we could devote the daylight hours to the pursuits we cared about. Sleep, apparently, was optional. We came in under cover of darkness and found our way to the forty-second floor, where for seven hours each night we waded through the thousands of pages of legal documents the firm produced each day.

Amid this drudgery thrived our merry band of nonconformists: Louie's quiet demeanor masked a passion for both jazz saxophone and tantric yoga (which we equated with hot, exotic sex—maybe even sex while playing jazz saxophone). He sometimes played his sax with his feet. Lynn explored vast expanses of expression by painting only still lifes, endlessly arranging gourds, funnels, pitchers, and pears on a table, always with a delicately folded tablecloth or napkin nearby. Nora knew more about new music and old movies than anyone I had ever met but still managed never to be a snob about it. She loved the comic strip *Nancy* and once convinced a group of us to pile into a pair of Dial cars when our shift ended at 7:00 AM and head up to the Museum of Cartoon Art in Port Chester, New York, for a special *Nancy* exhibit. (Dial was the limo service that the law firm provided to take graveyard employees home at the end of a shift, but the driver would take you wherever you asked. It was the early '90s, the era of corporate excess, and nobody was checking.)

And then there was Peter. Even within our group of artists, musicians, and misfits, he stood out. Peter was always spinning clouds and schemes. He wanted to swim with the dolphins. He wanted to study with Eiko and Koma, the iconoclastic Japanese performers who often performed by rivers or in the woods. He wanted to sail the seas on an old wooden ship, not just to imagine himself part of another time and place, but to make art out of the experience. Peter was a one-off, and I could not help but compare myself to him. After all, I had come to

New York to be an actor. Creativity was supposed to be my currency, but by the time I landed at Skadden in 1990 I felt no creative impulse at all. I had stepped away from the theater, and I had no plans to go back. I didn't see a way forward in that world.

I envied Peter. Whereas I felt I needed to be making a living as an actor (a goal at which I was failing), Peter made art out of anything, everything, and seemed content to take his audience as he found them.

"Norman is looking for people . . . "

It was Peter who found the boat, and a broken heart that led him to it. The woman he loved had left him in the winter of 1990, and he was determined to figure out why. What, he asked, could he learn from the experience? He was flipping through the catalogue of the Open Center—New York's one-stop shop for holistic healing—when he saw an ad inviting him to swim with the dolphins in the wild waters off Key West. It was January in New York. Peter was looking for something. Maybe he could find it in Florida. So he signed up, flew to Miami, spent one awesome night at a bar on South Beach—near the pretty girls—then on the beach itself. He saw blue water for the first time in his life. He collected bits of beautiful plastic in an array of colors, mostly aquamarine like the water, that he knew he would make art with someday.

The next day Peter rented a car and barreled across the bridges to the Keys, blasting Phil Collins's "In the Air Tonight" over and over as he drove. He arrived at Key West and embarked on his first full-blown New Age experience, complete with dolphin swims and partnered aquatic breathwork, all to the accompaniment of Enya and other transcendent tunes. For this working-class Catholic guy from Brooklyn, it was like stepping through the looking glass and finding a world he had hardly imagined, and he loved it. After several days of this, Peter was floating in the shallows with a group of fellow participants. The sun had begun its long descent, and the water, as he remembered it, "shone like shook foil. And I just felt like I was being rewoven into the fabric of the universe. It was a body sensation of having something great that I was a part of, and that was the cosmos."

Later, back on the catamaran sailboat that belonged to the retreat leader, Peter asked, if he wanted to continue this kind of work once he got back to New York, where should he start? The leader thought for a moment, then answered, "Well, first find a boat."

Upon his return, Peter set out to do just that. His graveyard shifts ended each Friday at 7:00 AM, when his weekend began. That next Friday he got home from work, slept for a few hours, then took the bus to the marina at Sheepshead Bay in Brooklyn. Starting at the first dock, he studied the boat moored there and quietly asked himself, "Is this my boat?" He stayed a few minutes before moving on to the next dock. Most were motorboats, recreational craft made of metal or fiberglass. Some were fishing boats, rusty and in need of repair. He did not talk to anyone, did not inquire about the particulars of each boat. He simply asked himself the question, waited for an answer, and moved on.

By the third week, Pete had looked at about two dozen boats and had run out of docks. He had made himself list a couple of possibilities, though he knew that none was his boat, if he was being honest. Feeling disheartened, he stopped in at the Stella Maris bait shop, picked up a fisherman's paper, and took in the place's "old salt" ambiance for a few minutes. Stepping back outside, he walked past the edge of Sheepshead Bay where it runs into Plumb Beach, the beach where his parents had brought him as a child. He took a few steps, then looked across the bay. And stopped. "A mirage," he said. "I thought I was seeing a mirage." It was a ship unlike any he had ever seen. With its sleek black hull and two masts that rose like great crosses from its deck, it looked as if it had sailed there not just from a distance but across time. Peter retraced his steps, passing all the boats he had looked at along the way. He hurried across the walkway to reach the Manhattan Beach side of Sheepshead Bay, running, stumbling, perhaps afraid that his vision had indeed been an illusion, the fallout of one too many graveyard shifts, and would disappear before he could find it again. Finally, out of breath, he arrived and stood transfixed, trying to take the measure of this magnificent ship.

Then, "Hello." An attractive dark-haired woman called to him from the deck. "Come aboard," she said.

Peter did not so much walk as float up the ramp to the deck of the ship, which he soon learned was the schooner *Anne Kristine* (pronounced "Anna Kristina"), the oldest continuously sailing vessel in the world. The woman was Mary Ann Baker. She and her family had found the ship in Tortola, in the British Virgin Islands, some years before, rebuilt her and sailed her back to New York. Peter told Mary Ann about his quest, and she said, "Well, why don't you come out on a half-day sail with us?"

Over the next several days Peter joined the Bakers two or three more times, once even going out on a stormy day, a mile or two off the coast of Coney Island. "When we got back, I felt like kissing the ground because I had been in a storm at sea," Peter said.

A friendship was growing. The Bakers told Peter that they were casting off for Nova Scotia. Would he come with them? As it happened, Peter already had plans to travel to Nova Scotia at just the time *Anne Kristine* would be there. Surely this was fate, the work of some greater power, of the cosmos. He had found his boat. He would meet them there. Peter flew to Bangor, Maine, with his friend Chris, who was coming off an Outward Bound experience and was up for any adventure. They found the ship and spent the day sailing with the Bakers, the cliffs of Nova Scotia in the distance. On their way back, they had to pass through Digby Gut, the narrow outlet that would bring them from the Bay of Fundy back into Annapolis Basin. It was a tricky stretch with strong currents, rocky ledges, and unpredictable winds. Captain Norman Baker asked Peter if he would like to take *Anne Kristine* through the Gut. Peter—scared and excited in equal measure—took the wheel, and, with Norman at this shoulder, navigated the schooner through the outlet. For the second time in as many months, and the second time in his life, Peter felt a higher power at work in his life, though this time the guidance was a little more literal. "I was at the helm, and I had to navigate to get through Digby Gut," Peter remembered. "And Norman's weathered, bearded face was about ten inches from mine. He was watching carefully, seeing to cosmic fair play as I brought his boat into the basin." For Peter, this meant he himself was in charge, literally at the helm, guiding a ninety-six-foot schooner through treacherous waters, the lives of those on board in his hands. But he wasn't doing it alone. Norman had his back—again, literally—bringing to bear his knowledge and experience and judgment to protect Peter and the other passengers and the ship. And guiding Norman was the very cosmos itself.

Peter was hooked.

"Norman is looking for people . . . "

"Oh," I said. "Really." I felt a grip in my gut. "That's nice." I understood why Peter was telling me this, why he expected me to share in his excitement. For him, *Anne Kristine* was no longer merely a ship, or even "his boat." She was the vessel of his deliverance, and a trip to Bermuda aboard her would surely bring him to the culmination of the quest. If guiding her through treacherous waters for a few minutes had given him a glimpse of a higher power, sailing her through blue water for eight days to the gateway of the Caribbean would certainly bring him nose to nose with the godhead itself.

My own relationship to the sea is a little more complicated, and as I listened to Peter my mind reeled back through the years, beginning with my birthplace. When I tell people I was born in La Paz, Bolivia, some of them know that Bolivia is a landlocked country in the heart of South America. Almost none of them know that it was not always landlocked. We lost our passage to the sea when Chile seized our coastal lands in the War of the Pacific in the late 1800s, a loss many Bolivians still perceive as nefarious. Bolivians have never forgotten and have never forgiven. Reclamation is part of our national identity. We still have a navy, our fleet of battered tankers and speedboats relegated to the country's Amazon-basin rivers and Lago Titicaca, the world's highest lake at twelve thousand feet above sea level. The flag of Litoral, as this lost coastal territory was called, still appears on calendars, posters, and other documents as the country's tenth province (we have only nine). Every March we mark the Day of the Sea, when politicians make promises and people listen to the recorded sound of seagulls. What happens to a people when they lose their passage to open water? Apparently, they are left with no access to the ocean but a longing for the sea.

It seems this longing did not come to much in my own family. The first time I saw the ocean was shortly after I arrived in the States. I was three, my brother Rob was four. My mother had a close friend, Barbara, who drove a convertible. One day they packed us boys into the backseat and took off for the shore. "Barbara took us to the bay near Annapolis," my mother later recalled. "There was a little beach there, and that was the first time you saw so much water." Rob and I stood at the lip of the sand, transfixed by the sound of the waves rumbling onto the shore, the expanse of the water, the strangeness of the terrain. Everything was strange. We had not seen our mother in a year, and we were not comfortable with her. Barbara was pale and blond and spoke a language we did not understand. She pointed at the little round-toed brown boots our grandmother forbade us to take off, ever. We never went barefoot. Finally, after much coaxing, we allowed Mami to take off our boots and socks, and we ventured a few steps onto the sand. It was too much for tender feet that never saw the light of day—a thousand hot pinpricks and ground that fell away before we could get our bearings. We screamed to be picked up and refused to go any farther, despite our mother's promises that the sand would be cooler by the water, the water would be nice. We never made it that far. We turned around and went home.

My mother was never comfortable in the water, and she wanted better for me, so on weekends she would take me to the community swimming pool near our house in Maryland. I would have preferred to be watching Saturday morning cartoons or lost in the latest *Peanuts* paperback; the sun, chlorine, and thrashing limbs usually overwhelmed me. We stuck to the shallow end, Mami coaxing me out to where I had to bounce on tippy-toes to keep my head above water. Swimming was out of the question. Whenever she tried to lift my legs and sustain me horizontally, I squealed and clung to her. Eventually she would tire, and we could go home.

Fast forward to July 20, 1969. When I woke up that day I was excited, though for the first few moments I could not remember why. It had been difficult to fall asleep the night before, and I was sure I had dreamed—good dreams, full of motion and power and flight, not the vampire nightmares that had begun to haunt me. I looked over at my dresser and saw my mostly authentic cardboard replica of the Apollo Lunar Module, a free giveaway from McDonald's that had instantly become my most prized possession. Of course! Apollo 11 had launched on Wednesday. We had watched liftoff on our family's first color television, and I had followed every detail of the mission. I knew that *Columbia* and *Eagle*, still attached, had entered lunar orbit the day before, July 19, at around 1:00 PM our time. They would orbit the moon thirty times before *Eagle* would separate and prepare to descend to the moon's surface.

Back on Earth, *Eagle* descended to the foot of my bed. I provided retro-rocket sounds and flattened the lunar surface to ensure a safe landing. Then, I remembered the rest of the reason for my excitement.

My family was going to Rehoboth Beach for the day (of course, we would be back in time for the moonwalk). I leapt from my bed to my big brother's. This day was too big to waste any of it alone.

We ran downstairs together, but the women in the family—our mother and grandmother—had long been up, getting ready for the trip. Mami was packing towels, sunscreen, spare clothes to change into. Abuela was in the kitchen. That was her domain, and everyone knew better than to trespass. She was putting the finishing touches on the sandwiches that would sustain us for the long drive. They were my favorite: ham and Swiss cheese on white bread, with mustard on one slice and mayo on the other. I was happy for the fruit she packed—apples, pears, oranges—and downright grateful for the bag of Lay's potato chips I knew we would soon be passing around.

Outside, Papi was going through his pretrip checklist—water, oil, tire pressure. He had bought the car from a friend who was ready to trade up, but for the life of me, I could not imagine what you could possibly trade up to from this: a 1963 Oldsmobile 88 (just six years past new), so many sleek lines I was sure it could fly if we went fast enough. It had a white top and a tan body, except for the right front fender, which was purple from when Papi had hit a deer and the auto body shop couldn't match the color. I took my place in the back, on the blanket that covered up some tears in the upholstery, with my brother, my mother, and my grandmother. My grandfather sat in front, and my father was at the wheel. This was the order of things.

Soon, we were on the road. A hot breeze came in through the open windows. I must have fallen asleep, because Mami woke me up as we were crossing the Chesapeake Bay Bridge, my favorite part of the trip. The car slowed down. Papi pulled into a large, blacktop parking lot and then into one of the few remaining spaces. It was still morning, but the heat came off the pavement in waves. Mami handed out towels and slathered sunblock on my arms, chest, and back. She helped me strap on my sandals (my brown boots were a distant memory). I stood and took my parents' hands. I looked to the left and saw my mother; I looked to the right and saw my father. My brother was with our grandparents. This was the world I knew, and these were my people. I looked up and saw the thin crescent of the moon against the pale blue sky, and I thought of the men up there. I tried to see the little speck that was them.

In the distance I heard a roar, and then a crash, again and again, in a rhythm with variations. I began to walk with my parents toward a sandy ridge; I could tell the sounds were coming from the other side. Impatient, I let go of their hands and ran up to the crest of the ridge, Abuela yelling after me, "¡Espera! ¡Ten cuidado!" There were people, and beyond the people there was water, first white water—the source of the sounds I heard—and beyond that blue-green water that stretched to the horizon. I had seen the ocean before, but somehow it felt different this time, as if I were part of a triangulation: from me, to the horizon, to the men circling the moon.

In that moment I could feel something in my chest that I did not fully understand. A small, quiet thought had taken hold: everything I knew to be true about myself and the world was no longer enough to hold this new information. It was as if I had gotten a glimpse of the universe, as if I had been made privy to a secret I could not have expressed even if I wanted to. There would be consequences, and though still a long way off, they would take me from my family.

I looked back. And then I ran, down the hill, across the beach, toward the water.

July 21 was supposed to be my first day of advanced beginner swimming lessons at Tallyho Swim Club, where my parents had signed the family up as members and where we rarely ever went. Despite its slightly pretentious, fox-hunt-derived name, Tallyho was nothing fancy. Nestled in a copse of trees up a small hill, the club included a regulation-sized main pool, a diving section with low- and high-dive boards, and a small wading pool, or "the baby pool," as everyone

called it. I enjoyed heading up to Tallyho with friends on hot summer
days, and I would have gone more often if I had been a swimmer. But
I rarely ventured out of the shallow end, and I could feel the panic
rise anytime my feet could not find the pool floor beneath me. So I
had felt both hope and fear when Mami told me she had signed me
up for lessons.

The first day of lessons was canceled because of the moonwalk.
Neil Armstrong stepped off the last rung of the lunar module's ladder
at just before 11:00 PM local time, and we—with millions of others
around the world—were watching. My lunar module landed at various spots around the family room before Abuela asked if I would sit
down and be still, please, and come watch history being made if I did
not want to go to bed. I sat. The problem was, there was not much to
see. One small fixed camera on the side of the module transmitted the
only live images any of us would see of this historic moment. Grainy
and washed-out, they revealed a ghostly figure as Armstrong made
the last small jump to the surface of the moon. Walter Cronkite spoke
for all of us when he let slip a small, "Wow," then gathered himself
enough to commemorate the moment more officially. "Armstrong is
on the moon," he said. "Neil Armstrong, thirty-eight-year-old American, standing on the surface of the moon." The specter on the screen
took a few steps before Armstrong uttered the famous "one small
step" line. It was thrilling.

Two days later, I found myself at the edge of the Tallyho pool with
a dozen other ten-year-olds, about to take my own giant leap. Well,
less a leap and more a few dainty steps into the shallow end, shiver-
ing in the early morning breeze. Looking back, it is hard to imagine
a creature more out of place than I felt. Whatever the converse of
a fish out of water is, that's what I was, scrapping to keep my nose
above the surface, unable to heed the instructor's pleas to relax as he
turned me on my back and held me as I looked up at the sky and
tried to hold back the tears. It was a long two weeks of lessons. The

whole thing seemed unnatural to me, especially putting my face in the water. Invariably, I insisted on taking a little breath while down there, presumably testing to see if the laws of pulmonary function still held true since the last time I had coughed up water. I would come up sputtering and flailing, and I would reach for a wall or an instructor or anything else to grab onto.

Despite my struggles, things did improve, and by the end of the two weeks I managed to tick off every course requirement. I could

- swim one length of the pool using an American crawl with rhythmic breathing,
- swim one length of the pool using an elementary backstroke,
- dive to the bottom of the deep end alone while holding my breath,
- do a rudimentary front dive (with a little help from the instructor), and
- do a survival float (or, as the instructor ominously called it, "a dead man's float") for two minutes.

Of course, that was all I could do. It was all so exhausting that once I was done with lessons, I had no desire to hang out at the pool like the other kids. On the last day, I got my certificate and hurried home. I walked in the door, threw down my towel, and said to Mami, "Gosh, I'm glad that's over!" She looked at me for a moment and said, "What do you mean 'over'? You're signed up for the intermediate class starting next week." I gave her a look I hoped would communicate just how ridiculous her suggestion was. Monday came, and I refused to go.

Fast forward again to April 13, 1981. It was my senior year at Davidson College, and I was on a picnic with friends at Lake Norman, the largest manmade lake in North Carolina. We were enjoying our last few weeks together; our coursework was over, and we could indulge in a weekday outing while our undergraduate pals sweated over finals. Someone had found a pulley on a line up a tree, and it led out over the water. Everyone was taking turns climbing the tree, grabbing the rope that hung down from the pulley, and riding the pulley out to the end of the line where it ended in a T. They would hit the T and let go, jettisoned out over the water, perhaps adding a flip before they splashed into the lake. They would then grab the rope that hung down and swim back, guiding the pulley back for the next person. Someone said, "Why don't you try it, Nelson?" I did not say no. I was a young man of twenty-two, out for a day with my peers, and saying no simply did not seem like an option.

So I climbed the tree and grabbed the rope. I jumped and swooshed down to the T, fell into the lake like a stone. I came up flailing, trying to find the end of the rope. At last I grabbed it and held on with all the strength I could muster while still trying to appear nonchalant to those on the shore. But when I tried to make my way back, I realized that my weight was forcing down the pulley so hard that it wouldn't move. My friends' trick had been to swim and lightly guide the pulley along the line. I panicked, let go of the rope, and started thrashing, trying to save myself. I was probably thirty feet from the shore, half that from a spot where I could have touched bottom, but none of that mattered. In that moment I forgot everything I had ever known about surviving in a water situation. Crawl, backstroke, dead man's float meant nothing to me. I was going under. And one thing to remember about drowning in a social setting is that, at least for a moment, your friends will likely think that you are joking. They will laugh and wave back, which is what my friends did before one of them realized this was no joke, plunged into the water, put me in a rescue hold, and pulled me back to shore. I sputtered my apologies, humiliated, while everyone looked on. But I could not say no.

Finally, my mind landed back in the present. Presumably, Peter was telling me about Norman's need for a crew because I had recently spent a week on the sloop *Clearwater*, "the boat that Pete Seeger built." The folk singer and activist devised the sloop as a way of bringing attention to the pollution of the Hudson River. For a twenty-five-dollar membership, you could sign up for one week as a crew member. I had paid up in the hope that Peter and I could sail together, but he'd had a conflict at the last minute, so I had gone alone. We sailed down the Hudson from Poughkeepsie to Tarrytown, New York, picking up groups of schoolchildren and teaching them about ships, sailing, and the stewardship of the river.

The onboard educator was a man named Rick Nestler. Rick reminded me of Quint, the cantankerous captain in *Jaws* played by Robert Shaw, albeit a much friendlier version. Rick did not so much seem like a sailor as someone playing a sailor. He was indeed both an actor and a seaman, as well as a singer and songwriter. The acting served him well when the kids came on board, as he could really throw himself into the telling of a tale, though sometimes he threatened to tip over into pirate pantomime. Rick's biggest achievement, though, was his song "The River That Flows Both Ways," an ode to the Hudson that became a staple of Seeger's performances. The song became our anthem that week, constantly requested and constantly played. It told a version of the river's early history and had the one nonnegotiable requirement of all good sing-along songs—an absolutely infectious chorus, which was sung twice in order to pick up anyone who might have been a little shy on the first go.

> *I could be happy just spending my days on the river that flows both way-ay-ay-ays!*

By the end of the week, there was not a shy one left among us. We were singing as if we were born to it and feeling like we were born to the sailing life as well—hoisting and swabbing, tying knots and casting off. It was all new to me, and though I did little more than follow instructions and try to be friendly (both of which came naturally to me), it felt like a great adventure. By the time we docked in Tarrytown, I had reconsidered the course of my life. I would give up my job as a legal proofreader, unshackle myself from my desk, and seek more honest work, preferably outdoors working with my hands. I determined to find out what positions might be available on the *Clearwater* itself. This feeling lasted as long as it took to get my land legs back. One of my mates drove me to the Tarrytown train stop. I took the next Metro-North train to Grand Central, then the subway back to Brooklyn. By the time I walked in the door of my apartment, the spell was broken. I felt tired and remembered that I was scheduled to work a graveyard shift at the law firm that night. I lay down and slept.

The *Clearwater* was as much of a sailing adventure as I craved, I realized. I had gotten to hoist a sail and feel the breeze push it along on a cool summer's night, to live out my swashbuckling fantasy of life on the high seas, all within the cozy confines of the Hudson River, always comfortably within view of the shore on either side, a fact that made all the difference to my feelings of safety and ease.

"Norman is looking for people to sail his ship to Bermuda."

This was different. Sail to Bermuda? That was open water. Blue water, in sailor's jargon. For days at a time. Peter kept talking, but I had stopped listening. I felt dizzy. "So," I said, "what's the deal?"

"I'm not sure," he said. "I'm going to call Norman to find out. I'll let you know." This was the first moment I could have protested. I could have called a halt to the proceedings and wished Peter luck. I didn't, and I've wondered about that ever since, given all that came after.

Later that evening a group of us waited for Peter outside the museum. I saw him walking along the sidewalk and hurried over so we could talk privately. He looked down as he walked, and the two enormous wool scarves he wore everywhere made him look a little like the Fourth Doctor in the *Dr. Who* series. He didn't see me until I was almost to him. "Petey!" I called. "What's up?"

"Bad news. Norman has a full crew. He doesn't need anybody."

I felt a jolt go through me. Released from the possibility of sailing to Bermuda, I was filled with the bravado of a man who has been denied the opportunity. It was the best of all possible worlds. I could say anything, and there would be no consequences. So, of course, I did.

"Oh, man, Pete. We would have been magnificent!"

I hugged my friend. He threw his scarves over his shoulder with a flourish, and we headed for our friends and the museum entrance. A weight had been lifted.

We walked into the museum. Mary Ann Baker came over and greeted us almost as if she had been waiting for us to arrive. "Hello, boys," she said. "What are you doing for the next two weeks?"

"Working."

"No," she said, "come sail with us. We're taking *Anne Kristine* to Bermuda, and we need more hands." She invited all of us.

Jonny said, "No, thanks. I can't."

I thought, *No.*

Peter said, "Yes!"

I thought, *No way.*

Mike said, "I'm in!"

I thought, *You must be joking.*

What I said was "Yes, yes, great."

Later I asked Jonny, "How could you pass that up?"

"I just didn't want to go."

So easy. But none of this had ever been easy for me. My family had learned early how to get along in this strange new land. Adjust, assimilate, accommodate. In our world, saying no did not have a high survival value. Every time I walked into a room, I raised a figurative finger to feel which way the emotional breeze was blowing, to know how to proceed. When I talked to people, I watched their faces closely to see how they were reacting to what I said. I could perceive the tiniest hint of upset or disapproval almost before they themselves were conscious of it. I would then subtly adjust my words until I got back in their good graces. It was an exhausting way to live, but one that had become second nature to me. When Mary Ann invited us to sail a 123-year-old tall ship from Brooklyn to Bermuda, I did not want to go. But I knew that I was supposed to want to go. And so I would go.

From then on, I was dead man walking.

We went in to hear Norman's talk. This lecture was about the craft called the *Tigris*, used for his third and last reed boat expedition with the explorer Thor Heyerdahl. I sat and listened as Norman described Heyerdahl's unorthodox theories of early human navigation and how they could explain the many similarities among civilizations separated by vast expanses of ocean. With the *Tigris*, Heyerdahl sought to make a connection between some of the earliest peoples—those of Mesopotamia, Egypt, and the Indus Valley. Norman was Heyerdahl's navigator and second in command, as he had been on the earlier expeditions. It was a journey of five months and four thousand miles. The crew of eleven crossed the Arabian Sea and encountered violence and unrest everywhere. The only port that would accept them was Djibouti—they could not get safe harbor anywhere else. So the crew decided to burn the *Tigris* as a protest and a plea for peace. A remarkable story.

Of course, by this point his narration was lost on me. My brain had shut down, with only reptilian functions—breath, heart rate, fight, flight—still engaged. I sat in the fifth row and looked up as each *National Geographic* image flashed on the screen, and I was on that boat. Forget *Anne Kristine*—I had Forrest Gumped myself onto the deck of the *Tigris* and sailed every one of those four thousand miles. I walked out of the theater exhausted, seasick, and rubber legged.

In the lobby the Skadden guys were talking to a slender, middle-aged man with a windburned face. This was Peter Abelman, a close friend of the Baker family and an experienced sailor. He would be the second mate on the *Anne Kristine* voyage. As I got within earshot, it became clear he was asking Mike and Peter about their sailing experience. My friends gave a little cheer when I appeared and pulled me into the conversation. Their excitement was palpable as they tried to impress Peter with their enthusiasm, if not their know-how. He smiled wryly as he listened, and I imagined him wondering what had gotten into the Bakers to make them invite these kids along. We three had "landlubber" written all over us.

After the museum, the four of us—Peter, Mike, Jonny, and I—went to a pub for a bite before our graveyard shift. As we waited for our food, I looked around the table for a sign that someone felt some of what I did. Yes, sailing to Bermuda on a historic tall ship was the stuff of boyhood fantasies, a not-to-be-missed adventure. But couldn't we acknowledge that it might also be the least little bit scary? And that, mixed in with our overwhelming feelings of excitement, there might also be a hint of anxiety, a dollop of doubt? And that these feelings, far from being a sign of weakness or lack of character, might be a wholly sensible reaction in the face of such a dangerous undertaking? Well, if anyone shared my consternation, he was not letting on. In fact, Jonny—the one guy who couldn't be bothered to go—had decided to stoke the excitement from the sidelines, exhorting us onward. And I was no better. Rather than try to steer us in a more reasonable direction, I seemed caught up in the rush. Every time I opened my mouth, I made it worse.

We arrived at the firm in time for our shift and proceeded to tell our supervisor that we would be out for the next two weeks because we were sailing to Bermuda. To our workmates, this was bigger than any legal brief they might be working on, and the proofreading room was abuzz with vicarious excitement. I wandered off in a daze. As I turned a corner, I ran into Nora, who knew me better than anyone else at Skadden. We often joked that we were siblings separated at birth, even though she is five years younger than I am. Nora possessed an intuitive sense about me that bordered on the prescient. As we passed each other in the hall, she didn't even say the words, she just mouthed, "Don't go." I wanted to fall at her feet and thank her, beg her to tell the others, to set me free. But I didn't. I couldn't.

And, yes, I understood that in some rational, objective world I could at any time have spoken up, raised a hand, said I'd changed my mind. This seemed about as likely as walking on the moon. I left before the end of my shift and headed home to Brooklyn to try to get some sleep. I was due at the boatyard in the morning.

———————

The next day, Thursday, October 24, Peter, Mike, and I made our way to Mill Basin, where the ship was in dry dock amid final preparations for the journey. Peter saw *Anne Kristine* first, at the far end of the yard. She was out of the water, and the scaffolding looked like two huge hands holding her up like an offering.

This would be *Anne Kristine*'s first trip without Norman at the helm. Busy with lectures and other commitments, he had hired a young sailor—Joey Gelband—to get her from Brooklyn to Bermuda. Norman would join the ship there to continue the trip to the Caribbean.

As we stood on the dock, Joey approached us. He had some bad news.

"We're eight," he said. "I need nine. I can only take one of you. I'll take the most experienced."

I bit my lip, trying to figure out what expression I should have on my face. Surprised? Quizzical? Expectant? Who knew? Inside I was *dancing a jig*, because I knew that, while Peter was a landlubber like me except for those few outings with the Bakers, Mike had been sailing his whole life—sunnies, daysailers, dinghies, all kinds of small craft. I shrugged in what I hoped looked like disappointment. "I've only had a week on the *Clearwater*."

Joey scratched his beard stubble. "Well," he said, "the *Clearwater* has the same kind of rigging as *Anne Kristine*. It's only a week, but you've still got more experience on a tall ship than these other two."

And so I would go.

Now, time seemed to speed up as I was pulled forward in the wake of my predicament. Two hours later I was on an Amtrak train to DC. I needed my passport, which was at my parents' house in Maryland. My parents were away, and my sister Fatima—fifteen years younger than me—was still at school. But my grandmother was home. Now, normally my grandmother was not one to be trifled with. But I was a man on a mission. I rang the doorbell. She opened the door, surprised to see me. She said, "What are you doing here?"

"Get out of my way, Abuela! I need my passport," I answered, as if that were all the explanation she needed. By this time I was on autopilot, because I could not allow myself to feel anything, much less think about the situation I had gotten myself into. I had to do this. I was going to do this. And if I let myself for a moment stop and think, it might be too much to bear. I got the passport, caught the next train back to New York, and spent a sleepless night in Brooklyn.

As I lay there, I thought back to meeting Norman for the first time. I had been in the museum lobby after the presentation, and Mary Ann had appeared at my shoulder with Norman in tow. He smiled warmly and shook my hand, told me how lucky they were to have someone with my experience aboard. Mary Ann informed Norman that no, I was not *that* Nelson, but I had volunteered for the trip. He let go of my hand and seemed to search for something to say, finally mumbled something I could not understand, then turned and walked away. I stood there with Mary Ann, a thin smile frozen on my lips. *Oh God*, I thought.

The next morning I packed a small bag and made my way back to Mill Basin.

2

NORMAN

———————

"I have dinosaur bones at my house because of my father."
—Mitchell Baker

THE LAST TIME I saw Norman Baker he looked just as vibrant as I remembered. His skin had that thin, papery quality that comes with age, but his eyes were just as keen, and piercing. They still made you feel you should weigh your words carefully before speaking. Not because he would criticize, but rather because you might disappoint him by offering inaccurate information or a poorly considered opinion. Surely, he would see through you, and you did not want to risk that.

I was presenting "The Accidental Sailor," the account of my experience on *Anne Kristine*, to the Hudson River Community Sailing school in fall 2016. Norman sat in the front row, scarcely six feet away, and he had no qualms about correcting me whenever he felt my account veered from the facts. It was a little unnerving.

Norman had not been easy to find.

When the school had invited me to tell my story as part of their speaker series that fall, I realized it had been almost twenty-five years since I had last shared that experience with anyone. Back then, just after, I would tell anyone who would listen. It was my way of working through the trauma, the numbness and shock of what I had been through.

Norman, it turned out, was a friend of the school, and the director gave me his e-mail address. I had not talked to Norman in almost as many years, not since, in fact, I had sat down to interview him at his home in Windsor, Massachusetts, in fall 1998. I was nervous about contacting him after all these years, anxious about what he would say. Would he resent someone dredging up this story again after so much time? I didn't need his permission, certainly. It was my own story I was telling, and I would tell it the best I could. But I did want something from Norman, I realized. I wanted his blessing.

I wrote him once, twice, three times without a reply. I tried not to take his silence personally as I debated what to do next. Then, an e-mail arrived. "Nelson, it was good to hear from you," it started. "I hope you'll excuse the long delay in responding. I was out riding, and my horse refused the last jump. I've been recovering." The man was eighty-eight years old. As our correspondence continued, I began to get a surprising picture of someone I had met twenty-five years earlier and known only a little.

In subsequent e-mails he wrote:

"This is being sent from San Diego, California. I flew here in my Skyhawk and will start flying home tomorrow. . . ."

"I think I told you I broke my neck last December and that has slowed down my social life though not my traveling. . . ."

"On the 15th I am boarding a heavy-metal flight to Norway where I will board a ship as a guest lecturer leaving on the 16th for Casablanca and then Brazil, the trip sponsored by the Kon-Tiki Museum. . . ."

"I'm guessing you don't know that I broke my hip skiing in Canada. . . . Had two titanium inserts realigning the pieces of broken bone. . . . One of the titanium inserts had to be removed and replaced by another of a different size and shape when the original piece managed to puncture the head of the ball joint and stab the socket. . . . That healing is actually going faster than anyone expected, and I do intend to participate in a canoeing/camping adventure in Saskatchewan. . . ."

I had known Norman as the owner and skipper of a nineteenth-century schooner, as an explorer and a scientist. If there were nothing more, he would have been among the most interesting people I had ever met. But clearly, there was more to the man than that. Something drove Norman Baker his entire life, an impulse that propelled him to prospect for gold in Alaska, climb the Matterhorn in Switzerland, set sail in a boat made of papyrus, not once but three times. He sought out brinks—both literal and figurative—again and again. He nearly died on numerous occasions and suffered a panoply of injuries great and small on countless others. He punched a shark.

Why did he do these things? Was he simply in search of a thrill? Was he an adventurer?

I put these questions to Norman once, sitting in the living room of his comfortable home in western Massachusetts. In answer, he told me a story. Once, in his twenties, he was on a pack trip with about a dozen others, traveling by horseback. After making their way across a wilderness area, they came upon a mountain called House Mountain and decided they would climb it. "We didn't have rope, carabiners, climbing shoes, pythons, nothing," he told me. "But we were just going to climb this mountain." One by one, the climbers dropped out. This was high enough for this one, high enough for that one. High enough for everyone except two of them: a young woman and Norman. "And like any young male, I wanted to impress this woman with my macho ability to climb this mountain when everybody else had dropped out," he said.

Eventually, they reached a point where the woman said enough, that was as far as she was going. It was too precipitous, too hazardous. Norman said he would look around the corner to see if there was a way to the peak, which was mere yards above them.

Norman saw that there was indeed a way to the peak, a ledge perhaps three inches wide at its narrowest. It spiraled up to a point where he could get his hands on the last craggy rock from which he could hoist himself to the peak. He looked down below the ledge and saw that the cliff was undercut. Below that, there was a talus slope, where rock that had broken off the mountain had rolled down to its angle of repose. The ledge would be easy enough to walk on. There were plenty of handholds. But there was a risk. "Maybe a piece of the ledge would break off. Maybe a handhold that I was depending upon would come loose," he said. The result would be certain injury and maybe death. Balanced against that was . . . nothing, really, except vanity. A chance to impress this young woman. He turned around and went back. "And I count that as the moment of my maturity," Norman said. "An adventurer would have gone up and probably would have made the peak and maybe would have died. And so, in that sense, I am not an adventurer. But I do enjoy adventure when the goal is worth the risk. That's the best way I can answer that question."

Later, Norman told me about a man who asked him to cross the Pacific in a vessel made entirely of inner tubes. When Norman asked him why he wanted to do this, the man replied that it had never been done before. Norman turned him down. To do something simply because it was dangerous and had never been done did not interest him, he told me. There had to be a greater purpose to the endeavor.

I don't understand what drove Norman to seek the experiences he did throughout most of his life. I'm not sure Norman fully understood either. It seems that people like Norman are too busy doing the things they do to sit around and contemplate why they do them. They leave that to more sedentary types. If I was an accidental sailor, someone who stumbled into an experience I could scarcely have imagined, Norman was the opposite. He was pure intent, a man who, by his own admission, could not stop something once he had started it.

Here, then, is a portrait of Norman Baker in a plane, a yacht, and three reed boats.

Norman Baker with *Anne Kristine* in the background. Photo by Mary Ann Baker

Norman always knew he would sail. As a boy growing up in Brooklyn, he rode his bike to Floyd Bennett Field on the borough's southern shore. There he would spend hours watching planes take off and land, and he would watch the ships. He was fascinated by the curvature of the earth, and how it seemed to draw the ships down—hull, deckhouse, smokestacks—each disappearing in turn, headed who knew where. Norman was determined to find out. "It wasn't a hope," he told me. "I just knew that someday I would sail to my heart's desire."

But first, he would fly. Norman entered a model-building contest sponsored by Piper Aircraft and assembled an exact replica of the J-3 Cub, the company's most popular light plane. He didn't win first prize (a four-year aeronautical engineering scholarship), but he did garner one of the consolation prizes: flying lessons. And so it was that Norman Baker, all of thirteen years old, first went up in the real thing—a Piper J-3 Cub. On his seventeenth birthday he soloed for the first time. It was a transformative moment. For the first time he felt free—free of the earth; free of the stolid, earthbound future that awaited him in Brooklyn; free to follow his dreams over the horizon.

In 1946, shortly after that first solo flight, Norman left for Cornell University. One of his roommates had been a fighter pilot during the war, and he seemed to sense a certain recklessness in this kid from Brooklyn. He told Norman to watch himself up there, that to avoid vertigo it was essential to maintain a visual reference or to have instruments that tell you "which way is up and which way is down."

One slightly overcast day, Norman took out his Piper Cub, the cloud ceiling no more than two thousand feet. As he gained elevation and flew through a few sparse clouds at the bottom of the overcast, the earth disappeared. He saw nothing but grayish-white. Suddenly, the earth reappeared and then was gone again. Fascinated by this aerial peekaboo, he thought of his roommate. And as he flew deeper into the clouds, he checked the only directional instrument the Piper Cub carried: a magnetic compass floating in alcohol. If he began to turn left or right, the compass would swing and he would correct his direction. By looking at the angle at which the compass floated, he could tell if the plane's nose was too high or too low.

He went into a climb, his heading steady, and flew up through the clouds, bursting through the cover. "All of a sudden there I was," he said, "on top of this layer of clouds, brilliant white beneath me and the bluest blue skies above." Above the cloud beds Norman found towers of cumulus clouds. He zoomed his Cub around these towers as if they were pylons, putting the plane into 180-degree turns with 90-degree banks. He had read J. G. Magee's famous poem of flight, and it came to him now,

Oh, I have slipped the surly bonds of earth
And danced the skies on laughter-silvered wings;
Sunward I've climbed and joined the tumbling mirth of
sun-split clouds, and done a hundred things
You have not dreamed of . . .

For Norman the dreaming was over. He was living this moment, and he was living it to the fullest. He flung his little Piper Cub around those "'footless falls of air,' yelling, singing, exuberant, just absolutely ecstatic." Then he decided to see how high he could fly. He put the plane into a climb and went up, and up, for minutes on end. Finally, he reached thirteen thousand feet, where the little plane seemed unwilling to climb any higher. The clouds were thousands of feet below.

Fair enough. It was time to descend. But how could he maintain the delirious magic of the moment? He would go down in a tailspin. Of course, he had never done a tailspin solo before, and when he had learned it, both he and the instructor had strapped on parachutes. This was a dangerous aerobatic maneuver, after all. This time he had no parachute, but "I was seventeen years old and immortal, so I just pulled the nose up, kicked the rudder and threw the plane into a beautiful tailspin." The sun was behind him, and every time the Cub came around, a golden flash sparked off the brass tips of the plane's wooden propellers. And then suddenly it was all gone.

He had spun down into the clouds, and now had to pull out with no visual reference. He knew how to pull out of a spin, so he did what he was supposed to do. He gave a rudder and thought he'd stopped the turning, but he couldn't be sure. So he popped the stick and pulled up. The airspeed should have come down; the altitude needle should have stopped. It didn't. The airspeed increased. Now he was feeling g-forces: two gs, three gs, four gs. His cheeks were being drawn down under his eyes. He thought maybe he'd fallen into a spin in the opposite direction. So he repeated the spin recovery routine from the other side. That didn't work. He tried it from the first side. The second side again. Nothing worked. The altimeter kept unwinding. The airspeed indicator kept going up. It passed the yellow line, the red line, and it finally went to the stop. The plane was at maximum indicated airspeed. It was shuddering, and the wings were shaking. The g-forces on his face were maxed out, and the breath was being pushed from his lungs.

In that moment, "I realized that I was going to die. And I told my mom and my dad that I was sorry. I knew I was taking myself away from them. I closed my eyes and waited for it to be over." Just then, the clouds tore away from in front of the windscreen, and the earth appeared dead in front of him. Now he knew which way was down. Jarred back to the moment, Norman used this new visual reference to stop his spin. He started to pull out of his dive but realized the new equation: the earth was approaching at a terrible speed, and if he didn't pull out in time, his Piper Cub would slam headlong into the ground; at the same time, the plane was shuddering beyond all reckoning, and pulling up too quickly could shear the wings off.

If you're going to be an explorer, and skirt death more than once, and eventually sail across the Atlantic in a boat made of papyrus, and live to tell your grandchildren about it, there is one quality you had better exhibit, and that is an inability to panic. When faced with a crisis, Norman Baker always reduced things to essentials: evidence and conclusions, cause and effect. In this moment, in a very real sense, the sudden and violent meeting of earth and machine, or loss of wings, became incidental. Norman would methodically do what he knew to do, and it would yield results, or it would not. He knew that he had to lower the horizon, which was over his head, down to the front of the plane. He pulled back on the stick, checked the wings, checked the horizon.

Pulled back again. Check. Check.

Repeat.

Of course, this entire process probably took as long as it took to read that last long paragraph. To survive such a moment you must go slow, and fast. You must act in a heartbeat while imagining you have all the time in the world. You must test the elasticity of time.

In the next instant the horizon was in front of him, his fuselage was parallel to the ground, and he was headed home.

Later, Norman told his pilot friend about what had happened. The friend said, "You were in a graveyard spiral. You're a stupid kid and you should never, ever try that again." He never did.

———————

Norman's first job after college took him not to the sky or the sea but to the desert. Working for the El Paso Natural Gas Company, he was part of a team that surveyed the boundary between Colorado and New Mexico. They traveled by horseback and carried their supplies by mule, camping out for weeks at a time. When they finally returned, Norman learned that North Korea had invaded South Korea, and that American troops were being dispatched to help the South Koreans.

Norman had joined the naval reserve while at Cornell, and he was called up. He was assigned to a destroyer and spent the next two and a half years off the coast of North Korea. At twenty-three he became the navigator on a two-thousand-ton steel vessel driven by sixty-thousand-horsepower engines and crewed by 330 men. "I told it where to go," he said. They went out on monthlong patrols, looking for targets of opportunity. They fired thousands of tons of shells and took a few hits themselves, losing several men. Norman's gums bled incessantly, and a navy dentist told him it was because he had been clenching his teeth so hard for so long. It was not what he'd imagined when he had watched the ships disappear over the horizon as a child. Toward the end of Norman's service, one of the destroyer's radar-men overheard Norman grumbling that this wasn't the experience of the sea he'd had in mind. "Well, Mr. Baker," he said, "you're on the wrong kind of ship. You don't want a steel ship run by steam. What you need is a wooden ship driven by the wind."

After his discharge, Norman caught a flight from Japan to Hawaii to make his way home. As luck would have it, a transpacific yacht race was then ending in Oahu, and he joined hundreds of others for the climb to Diamond Head to watch the finish. It was night, and huge aerial searchlights shone on the water. Out of the darkness, a magnificent white yacht appeared. With every sail set, she had a bone in her teeth, pushing the seas aside with a great white bow wave on either side, and a wake that boiled out behind her and streamed into the dark. Norman thought of the radarman. Yes, a wooden ship driven by the wind. The yacht was *Circe*, a seventy-five-foot cutter, and her skipper Ray Cook had built her to last. For her hull he had used cured oak decking from scrapped World War I battleships. He had added a seventy-five-foot cast-iron keel on the outside and concrete ballast to cement her ribs on the inside. She was magnificently strong.

The vision of *Circe* helped shape Norman's desire to sail into something like a plan. He would not simply sail; he would sail around the world. This phrase, "to sail around the world," would define the rest of Norman Baker's life and dictate every decision he would make from that moment on.

But first he had to get on the water. He approached Ray Cook, and Cook saw enough in him to overlook his lack of yacht-sailing experience. Certainly, his naval experience and his skill as a navigator weighed in his favor. More than this, however, was Norman's seriousness. He was young, but he was no kid. Cook could tell that Norman would be a good man to have by his side.

Cook took Norman on for his next transpacific race. This one would go west to Papua New Guinea, and it would be the first leg of Norman's circumnavigation. But the race was a disaster, turbulent seas wreaking havoc with many of the yachts, including *Circe*. They came

in last in their class, and most of Cook's crew, who had agreed to help
him sail back to Seattle, abandoned him. Norman was not supposed to
sail back on *Circe*. His plan was to continue west, around the world.
But when Cook asked him to stay on, Norman agreed.

The two set off for Seattle with a young, inexperienced crew, the
only one they could find. They got as far as Hawaii, but Ray Cook
became ill and nearly died at sea, and Norman just managed to reach
Honolulu. After two weeks in the hospital Cook recovered, but he was
too weak to go on. Since 1932 *Circe* had never left the dock without
Cook aboard. Now he asked Norman to take her home. Norman was
twenty-six years old. He did not want to be a captain, didn't feel ready.
He certainly didn't want to take the love of this man's life across the
Pacific. But Cook pleaded, and Norman finally agreed.

Norman set sail, again with a mostly young, inexperienced crew
of five, only one of whom had ocean-sailing experience. Several days
out of Hawaii the wind died, and they began to motor through a calm.
They reached the edge of the calm just after dawn when the sea, which
had been glass-smooth, began to curve into swells, long swells that
indicated a storm in the distance. By the afternoon, the wind began
to rise, and the swells became waves. By six o'clock that evening, the
winds had grown to gale force. Long, steep waves lifted *Circe*, and
she was gaining speed on the downhill side of each wave. They shut
off the engine and put up two headsails to give the boat steerageway,
to keep her moving and responding to the movement of the rudder.

Steering a sailboat in these conditions takes skill, strength, and
stamina; you're fighting not only the force of the waves and wind but
also the tendency of the craft to broach, to turn sideways to the sea.
If that were to happen in these conditions, the boat would capsize.
Of their crew, only Norman and his first mate, Van, were qualified to
be at the helm in this storm. Norman would take the first shift until
midnight while Van rested. Van would steer from midnight to dawn.
At midnight Norman sent one of the young crew members down to

call Van up to take his watch. Norman stayed with his mate for a few minutes to make sure Van was acclimated; then he went below to his bunk and fell in.

Soon the sound of heavy footsteps in the corridor woke him, and Norman looked out to see the big figure of the first mate standing there. Norman leaped out of his bunk and shouted, "Van, is that you?"

Van turned and said, "You can't hold it."

"Van, who's steering?"

"You can't hold it. You just can't hold it."

"Who's steering?"

Van then lay down on his own bunk, still in his foul weather gear and his seaboots. He crossed his hands across his belly and looked up with vacant eyes, repeating, "You can't hold it, you just can't hold it."

Norman raced to the deck in his skivvies. There he found one of the young crew members clutching the wheel as he steered the boat down the face of thirty-foot waves, eyes like saucers, saying, "I don't know what to do. I don't know what to do. Help me, help me, help me." Norman took the wheel and told him to fetch his foul weather gear. He steered until morning, by which time the wind was blowing so hard that it threatened to blow out the headsails. "All hands on deck," he called. Every man tied on, life jackets all around. He ordered them to take down the jib.

Just then, everything disappeared. Norman fell, hitting his head against the steering wheel as his body slammed against the deck. He found himself on his knees with water swirling around his armpits. Raising himself up by the steering wheel, he felt warm liquid on his face, blood running down across his left eye where his brow had been cut. Looking down, he saw only white foaming water around his waist. A coconut floated in the water to his right, and he remembered that they had had a box of coconuts lashed down on the deck. He got his bearings and looked farther out, and he saw . . . nothing. No rail, no deck, only the horizon. "There was no ship," he told me. "I was standing in the sea, and there was nothing to be seen but the mast of the ship sticking up out of the water like a submarine's periscope, and men floating in the water in their life jackets, struggling to get back to the mast." *Circe* had been buried by the sea.

They had been hit by an augmented wave—aptly known as a rogue wave—which occurs when two normal waves get out of phase and create a wave twice as large. Worse, Norman had failed to fasten the main hatch, and it had slammed open when the wave struck. Beneath his feet, he could feel the water thundering down into the ship, filling it. Norman waited, counting the seconds. He knew the period of the waves, how long between the crests. And he knew that when the next crest came, it would finish them. He'd always wanted to go to sea, and now he would stay there. The seconds passed, but the wave did not come. He counted—still nothing. The subsequent wave had been canceled, as sometimes happens with an augmented wave. They had twice as long between the crests, and in those extended seconds, *Circe* surfaced. "The sea rose before me, it bulged. Suddenly there was this huge ridge in front of me with great tons of water pouring off to both sides. Finally, *Circe*'s bow came rearing up out of the sea like a surfacing submarine and fell onto the surface with a great slam. And I thought, *My God, we're floating.*"

Then the next wave did come. Would *Circe* rise to it or be swamped by it? She tilted forward as the water inside her cascaded into her bow, lightening the stern. The stern rose to the wave. The wave crashed and tumbled beneath them. *Circe* had ridden the wave. She could float. "The pumps!" roared Norman. "Man the pumps!" The crew slammed the hatch shut and manned the pumps. It took them most of the day to get all the water out of *Circe*, but they made it.

Ten days later they sailed into Puget Sound.

———

Some might have seen this experience as a sign to seek drier, more land-bound endeavors. For Norman it was a sign of a different kind. "It almost seemed as if I had been given a precious gift," he said, "an education in how to manage myself at sea. And I hadn't paid a terrible tuition for it." He hadn't lost any men. He hadn't lost the ship. He never doubted he would go back. "It almost seemed ungrateful not to." He spent only a week in Seattle before seeking his next opportunity to do just that.

Part of Norman's agreement with Ray Cook was a plane ticket back to Hawaii. Once back on the islands, he soon met John Ernest Randall, an American ichthyologist. Jack Randall would go on to become a world authority on coral reef fishes, but in 1955 he was a young man with a newly minted PhD, a wife and child, and a grant to study a type of grouper fish in the South Seas. He also had a ketch that was built for sailing in bays, not the ocean. Buoyed by his recent adventures, and unswayed by the ketch's limitations, Norman agreed to be Randall's navigator—and entire crew. Between the two of them—and with Randall's wife, Helen, and three-year-old daughter, Laurie, aboard—they made their way to the Society Islands, to places with names like Huahine, Raiatea, Mo'orea, "as if they'd been named by poets rather than cartographers, the water so clear you could count your toes five feet down."

After Randall established himself in Mo'orea and started conducting his research, he recommended Norman to the captain of *Te Vega*, a 125-foot steel-hulled commercial schooner that worked all over the South Seas. He also introduced his young navigator to Thor Heyerdahl, the Norwegian explorer who had sailed his raft *Kon-Tiki* to those islands from South America a few years before.

Norman joined *Te Vega* as a deckhand on a ship that plied the seas of Polynesia, transporting cargo between Hawaii and the South Sea islands. He rose to first mate in a remarkable six months, a progression that normally took years. It was an idyllic time. "Most of the crew were Tahitian," he said, "and wherever we docked we were greeted like family." Norman was struck by the warmth of the Polynesian peoples, by their strong family ties. And he was smitten by their children. "They were charming and spontaneous. They played with simple toys like shells or nuts or carved pieces of wood. They were lovable in every sense of the word."

The experience awakened in Norman a feeling that had been growing, perhaps since the time he had spent with Jack Randall and Helen and Laurie. As much as he craved a life at sea and a chance to explore the world, he realized he now wanted something even more. He wanted to be a father, and he knew it was never going to happen bumming around the world on sailing ships. So it was that, when offered the captaincy of *Te Vega* at age twenty-seven, he turned it down. Instead of sailing west, around the world, he made his way east, back to Brooklyn, to the life he had left behind.

———

Norman had been writing to his brother Howard, who was working in Austria as an engineer. Both men loved to travel, and neither wanted to be tied to a conventional employer "who would only be willing to give us two weeks flat out." They would work for themselves in the family's construction business. As Norman put it, "One guy could stay home and manage the store. The other guy could take off for months at a time."

Soon after returning to Brooklyn, he met Mary Ann Tischler. "It was just a date originally," said their youngest son, Mitchell. No Hollywood meet-cute scenario, just two young, attractive people looking for a suitable partner in late '50s New York. She was from Washington Heights in upper Manhattan; he was from Crown Heights, Brooklyn. They married a year later. An unremarkable start, perhaps, but it would lead to a remarkable partnership. Mary Ann may have lacked

Norman's experience—she was twenty-one when they met—but she matched his adventurous spirit. She understood that this impulse made life worth living for him. It wasn't long before sailing around the world became a regular topic of conversation for the young couple. And like her new husband, when she started a project, she never gave up. Moreover, Mary Ann possessed qualities that Norman lacked, qualities that complemented his. Where Norman could be irascible and socially awkward, Mary Ann was a charmer, a beautiful, gracious woman who made everyone feel welcome. As Mitchell put it, "My mom gave my father a social life outside of adventurers. My father could get along with the Thor Heyerdahls of the world, but they're a rare breed. My mother could get along with all the other people in the world."

The two married in 1960; Daniel, their first child, was born in '61. A favorite aunt of Norman's half-jokingly informed them that all the fun was over because raising children was a full-time job. Elizabeth was born in '62. When they bought a house in New Rochelle in 1963, Mary Ann was pregnant with their third child. One day, Norman came home to find Mary Ann in tears. She had just finished reading James Michener's book *Hawaii*, and she was afraid they would never get away. With three children and a mortgage, how could they even consider something so irresponsible? That night they made a pact: whatever their circumstances, in ten years they would simply sell everything, take their children, and go. This promise allowed them to devote themselves to their present life. Norman built the construction business with Howard; Mary Ann devoted herself to caring for the children and studying to earn her master of education degree; together they worked at making their house into the home they wanted. They knew their day would come.

Norman's day came sooner than expected. In late 1967 he sat down to lunch with Thor Heyerdahl in New York City. Heyerdahl was preparing for his next expedition, and he thought Norman might be right for the team. Norman had thought about the Norwegian often since they first met in Tahiti years before. He admired Heyerdahl, even considered him a role model. After all, the explorer had forged a life out of the two elements Norman himself most longed for: adventure and purpose. But when he heard what Heyerdahl was planning, it was too much. Cross the Atlantic in a reed boat? Norman could see crossing the ocean on a balsa log raft, as Heyerdahl had done on *Kon-Tiki*. Each log on that vessel had been a foot and a half in diameter. Now Heyerdahl wanted to traverse the Atlantic on a boat made from reeds whose largest diameter was "the size of your forearm and the smallest was the size of your finger." This was madness. But they talked deep into the night. Norman challenged Heyerdahl's calculations. He questioned his suppositions. Heyerdahl had an answer each time. By the end of the dinner, Norman was convinced.

Heyerdahl had first seen the papyrus boats in Egyptian hieroglyphs on a visit to the Museum of Cairo. They reminded him of drawings he had seen of boats built by indigenous people of the Americas. He began to research these similarities and found more than a hundred archaeological and cultural matches between civilizations that existed independently, separated by thousands of miles of water. The similarities were uncanny. Was it not possible, he asked, that the inhabitants of Mediterranean civilizations might have crossed the sea thousands of years earlier than supposed? Not on wooden ships, of course (this era would come later), but on boats made of reeds tied up with rope, driven by sails made of Egyptian cotton and steered by cedars of Lebanon. Heyerdahl was roundly ridiculed at every conference where he presented this idea. He decided that, if he could not prove definitively that the crossings had happened, he could demonstrate that they were possible.

Would Norman join him? He struggled with his feelings. It had been ten years since his days in the South Pacific. He ached to be back at sea, to feel that alive again. Beyond that, he realized that if the expedition were successful, he would have a hand in changing a vital part of our understanding of human history and the connections people had made before wooden ships made those crossings more feasible. And he would love to rebuke the narrow mindset of Heyerdahl's critics. But Norman's life had changed. "When I met him in Tahiti, I was young, single, unattached," Norman recalled. "If he wanted to go by papyrus boat to the moon, I'd say, sure, I'll get my toothbrush." As he arrived home that night, he was afraid the chance had come too late. He told Mary Ann about the crazy proposition Heyerdahl had made to him. She listened. Then she told him the proposition wasn't crazy. She told him he was crazy if he didn't go. She thought he was working much too hard and needed a vacation. "And Mary Ann, who had never been to sea, thought that this would be a vacation for me."

And so he would go.

Norman and Heyerdahl began to plan. Both men understood well the dangers of the sea, so they made a list of every hazard that might befall them out there, then promised themselves they would not set sail until they had devised a way out of every hazard. Man overboard, fire onboard, storms. They came up with twenty-one hazards and twenty-one ways out. Then, they came up with *two* ways out of every hazard. In the year and three months between the time they decided to go and the time they left, Norman often wondered if joining this voyage made any sense. He thought about *Circe* and the navy and his time with Jack Randall, about the times he had almost not come back from the sea. His knees would shake and the cold sweats would come, and he would sit down and pull out the list. Was there any hazard not on the list? He couldn't think of any. What about the ways out—were they reasonable? He would work his way down the list, questioning each point. As he worked through this ritual, he could feel his pulse quiet, his chest soften. He would be OK. Then, in a week or two or three, he would have to do it again. He consulted that list until the day they shoved off, when he finally tore it up and threw it away.

The vessel, christened *Ra* to honor the Egyptian sun god, was built by Buduma boatbuilders from Lake Chad in central Africa. Heyerdahl had twelve tons of papyrus transported from Lake Tana, the source of the Blue Nile, to within sight of the Great Pyramids near Cairo. Local potters working in the ancient manner created 166 jars to store water and provisions. Once the boat was built, five hundred physical education students hauled *Ra* across the Egyptian desert to the nearest road, where the boat was taken by truck to Alexandria, then by ship to the ancient Moroccan port of Safi.

Heyerdahl, as much aware of symbolic significance as of scientific purpose, assembled an international crew to represent the expedition's sense of cooperation and common purpose. They would sail under the flag of the United Nations. *Ra* departed from Safi on May 25, 1969, with a crew of seven. Besides Norman and Heyerdahl, the crew consisted of Carlo Mauri (Italy), Yuri A. Senkevich (Russia), Santiago Genoves (Mexico), Abdullah Djibrine (Chad), and Georges Sourial (Egypt).

They were bound for Barbados. Within an hour, a huge swell had smashed both rudders. It was a problem that would plague them the entire trip. Whenever it stormed, one or both rudders broke. In retrospect, Norman felt they had misinterpreted the ancient Egyptian builders' models and drawings, which depicted the boats with enormous rudders the size of telephone poles. Certainly, they thought, the artists who had created the drawings had just been clumsy; nobody could want something that big on a boat so small. "But that's exactly what was needed," said Norman. "Our rudder shafts were much too slender. Whenever we tampered with the ancient design, we paid for it."

Another mistake they paid for involved the shape of the boat itself. In the Egyptian hieroglyphics both ends of the boat were turned up, with a line connecting each end to the mast, but the Buduma boatbuilders had never built a boat with an upturned stern. Only the front end of the boat should be turned up, they said. If you put two front ends on the boat, which way would it go? Norman tried to explain to them that on the ocean you had to move hills of water, and that the two-bowed shape would help. The Buduma boatbuilders had never seen a wave and thought they were being teased. The builders went on strike, refusing to touch the boat for four days. At last they relented, only to cut the rope that held the upturned stern in place, saying it served no purpose.

Ra held up for several weeks. Once they reached the trade winds, they made steady progress. Storms damaged the masts and the sails, and regularly broke the rudders, but the crew managed to keep up with repairs. Norman and Heyerdahl's hazard list had prepared them to respond to every situation. They were pleased that, while the boat's wooden parts broke constantly, the papyrus held up exceedingly well. Eventually, though, the stern began to wilt, then sink below the ocean's surface. Waves washed on board, and the boat sailed lower in the water each day. Finally, they lost one of the blades of their oft-repaired rudders in a squall. With only one blade, it was impossible to steer. They broached, turning sideways to the oncoming waves. The yard, the spar from which the sail was set, slammed against the mast and cracked. They were buffeted by the waves. The seas slammed over the sides and began to tear *Ra* apart.

They issued an SOS to the amateur radio operators who had been following their progress, asking their help in finding a ship to rescue them. Even so, it was another eight days before they managed to raise a vessel on their hand-cranked radio. The yacht *Shenandoah*, out on a charter, finally spotted them and approached. Half of *Ra* was underwater, and sharks had begun to circle. Norman and the rest of the crew salvaged all they could, then watched as the remaining papyrus drifted off. They were a week shy of Barbados.

The *Ra* expedition quieted some of Heyerdahl's critics. Though he and his crew had not reached land, they had shown that a reed boat built using ancient designs could indeed traverse the ocean. But others continued to disparage *Ra*'s accomplishments, accusing the crew of using modern methods. This rankled Norman, who often found himself responding to these quibbles. What modern methods? he asked. The use of cameras, film? Those just weighed them down. Radios? Those helped them be found. They did not drive the ship through the water. Navigating instruments? How bad a navigator would you have to be to miss the entire western hemisphere?

Still, to come so close without completing the mission was a difficult pill to swallow for the entire crew, especially as they felt they had learned from their mistakes and would not make them again.

Within two months, Heyerdahl proposed a second expedition, and most of the original crew jumped at the chance to go. The explorer had noticed that the reed boats built by the Aymara Indians of Bolivia and Peru most resembled the Egyptian hieroglyphics, with an upturned bow and stern. Heyerdahl's new craft would follow this model; in fact, he brought four Aymara boatbuilders, all from the same family, from Lake Titicaca to Morocco to supervise the building of the boat. The four, Demetrio, José, Juan, and Paulino, were accompanied by an interpreter, Señor Zeballos, a museum curator from La Paz. (I met the family by chance on a trip to the lake some years later. Their role in the making of *Ra II* had become a part of their community's lore, and pictures of the undertaking were displayed in the small museum on Isla Suriqui, where they lived. When I pointed to Norman and said that I knew him, it was a matter of celebration. They insisted on fetching the one surviving brother who had worked on the project— Paulino, I believe—and explaining to him that I was a friend of Norman's. Pictures were taken. I promised to say hello to their friend.)

Besides its shape, the length of *Ra I* had been an issue. One of the reasons that *Ra I* had come apart was because it flexed so badly in the waves. Once they were at sea, Heyerdahl remarked that the waves were nothing like the long, low waves he had experienced in the Pacific. Norman explained to him that because the Atlantic is half the size, wavelengths are shorter and steeper. At thirty-nine feet, *Ra II* was about ten feet shorter than its predecessor, sixteen feet wide at its center, and six feet deep. Its double-cylinder hull was compact and inflexible, "rigid as a block of wood," as one crew member put it. And this time they had rudders the size of telephone poles.

Ra II launched from Safi on May 17, 1970, and began sinking almost immediately. Within two weeks, the boat had sunk two feet, and only twelve inches of deck remained above the water. "You didn't have to be a rocket scientist to realize that in three weeks it would be decks awash," remembered Norman. "The voyage would be ended, a much more ignominious failure than the previous year." The crew were all so embarrassed that they didn't even want to radio for help. Instead, they hoped to reach the Cape Verde Islands, about twelve hundred miles from their starting point. There they would quietly quit. They began throwing things overboard to lighten the load: food they would not be afloat long enough to eat, water they would never drink, repair materials, tools. They even threw over the only life raft they had on board, a papyrus dinghy. To their surprise, *Ra II* then stabilized. Was it the lightening of the boat? Or was there some formula for getting a certain volume of reeds underwater? Whatever it was, the Cape Verde Islands came and went, and *Ra II* kept sailing.

She arrived at Barbados late on July 14, escorted by a flotilla that included fishing boats, pleasure boats, and a replica of the pirate ship *Jolly Roger*. Prime Minister Errol Barrow flew out on a small plane and circled them. The crew sailed along Barbados's South Coast and into Carlisle Bay, finally making their way to Blackwood Screws Dock, where the little reed boat was lifted out of the water. A crowd of hundreds of Bajans greeted the travelers as they set foot on land after a journey of fifty-seven days and 3,270 miles. Heyerdahl, Norman, and their comrades at sea were stars.

The *Ra* expeditions made Norman famous, or something like it, and changed the Bakers' trajectory forever. *Ra I* made the news; *Ra II* made the cover of *National Geographic*. For an explorer, it did not get any bigger than that. (For years after, Norman graced the back cover of magazines as well, in a Rolex ad. The ad featured Norman in the foreground holding a sextant and with a watch on his wrist. In the background, *Ra II* appears, half submerged after having taken a wave. The caption: "3,270 miles across open ocean. A cruel test for a papyrus boat. An easy trip for a Rolex.") After the *Ra* expeditions, the world that Norman so longed for and wanted to share with his family came through their door. Thor Heyerdahl and the rest of the international crew visited—African, Russian, Egyptian, Japanese. For children living in 1960s America, these visits were revelatory. Even the expeditions' mascots, Sinbad the duck and Safi the monkey, lived in the backyard for a time. Mitchell, only five when Norman left for the first voyage, grew up with the expeditions, his childhood framed by his father's absences and the rewards that came from being his child. "The fact that I knew what papyrus was, that I knew where Lake Titicaca was, I loved all that," he told me. "I have dinosaur bones in my house because of my father."

Elizabeth, six years old when Norman left for the first *Ra* expedition, remembered little about it, but she did recall a story Mary Ann often told about her first night alone with her children after Norman had left for Africa. The phone rang; it was Norman's father, and he was furious. Edward Baker told her that if anything happened to his son, he would never forgive her. Why hadn't Mary Ann stopped him from going? She had never considered it. Elizabeth said, "I felt like my mom was really the perfect partner for my dad because she didn't hold him back. She knew that to be out in the world and explore the world and journey in the way he needed to was an important part of who he was. And that became important for her as well. They had a real partnership, even though I think her part was more difficult. But it was a partnership."

Several years later, their partnership would be tested again when Heyerdahl summoned Norman for one last reed boat journey. The *Tigris* cast off from the river Shatt al-Arab in Iraq in late 1977 with three mates returning from the *Ra* expeditions—Norman, Carlos Mauri of Italy, and Yuri Senkevich of Russia—and eleven crew members in all. As with the earlier excursions, Heyerdahl sought to demonstrate that ancient civilizations—in this case those of Egypt, Mesopotamia, and the Indus—could have had contact across the seas that separated them. This time Heyerdahl and his colleagues confronted more than natural dangers; they sailed a sixty-foot reed boat with no engine and no defenses through some of the world's most troubled waters, past Iran, Pakistan, Oman, and Yemen. They traversed the Persian Gulf, the Gulf of Oman, and the Arabian Sea. At one point they confronted an Omani gunboat from which ragged-looking seamen pointed a .50-caliber machine gun at the *Tigris*. The Omani commander asked the crew if they were ghosts. He could imagine no other explanation for the sudden appearance of this ancient vessel.

Elizabeth, then fifteen, was old enough to know that her father was sailing in a dangerous, unstable part of the world. She was worried. War had broken out between Ethiopia, Eritrea, and Somalia, and the family calculated that the *Tigris* was sailing in the waters off the Somali coast. One afternoon, Elizabeth was home alone. The telephone rang, and when she answered it, she heard a voice on a crackling phone line shouting, "The ship is burning! The ship is burning! *Tigris* is burning!" She told me, "I remember thinking, *That's it. My dad is dead.*"

Later, she learned that the boat had reached the Bab-el-Mandeb Strait, the Gate of Tears, the entrance to the Red Sea. Heyerdahl wanted to enter here, then sail the length of the Red Sea to Egypt to complete the journey from ancient Mesopotamia. When *Tigris* requested passage, the crew was told that if they came within two miles of any of the combatants' coasts, they would draw fire. A French commercial airliner had wandered into that zone and been shot out of the sky by

Somali jets. Everyone aboard had perished. The French government had sent out a search-and-rescue plane to look for survivors. That plane, too, was shot down and everyone aboard killed.

When Djibouti offered *Tigris* safe harbor, the crew decided they would go no farther. On April 3, 1978, after five months and 4,200 miles, they set *Tigris* ablaze as a protest against war and a plea for peace. "The person on the line didn't know that," Elizabeth said. She never found out who the caller was.

The *Tigris* voyage would be Norman's last excursion with Thor Heyerdahl.

What was that first day back like for Norman? He had been away almost six months, had been cut off from his wife and children entirely except for the occasional radio communication. Had his wanderlust been satisfied, at least for the moment? Was he ready to get back to normal family life? Of course, life at the Baker house had never been "normal." That just was not who Norman was, or Mary Ann either. Family vacations included a steady stream of hiking, camping, canoeing, kayaking, sailing, horseback riding. The three kids were on skis by the time they were walking. Winters were spent at the family cabin in western Massachusetts, where Norman was a ski patrolman. Norman, the born explorer, wanted his family to experience life as something you *did*, not something you sat through. For the most part, this made for good family outings, though youngest child Mitchell would have enjoyed an occasional visit to an amusement park. Instead, the family hiked the White Mountains, "where no one else got to see," his father would say. "Until one day the Cog Railway came up," Mitchell remembered, "and I saw a chubby little kid eating an ice cream. And I hadn't had an ice cube in a week. That was one of the early betrayals of being Norman's child."

Small betrayals aside, being a Baker had its benefits. "I loved it," said Mitchell. "I liked being the different family." They were a little like an astronaut's family. For long stretches they lived a typical suburban life. Then their father would go away, and when he returned things would be different, though not always in ways that were easy to define. He would be changed, and the family's life would pivot. The kids knew they were part of something bigger and more exotic than what most other families in Westchester were doing. Their father appeared in the local paper. He lectured at the local schools. Eventually, the demand grew, and Norman's speaking engagements became a part of the whole family's routine. "We didn't have a lot of money," remembered Mitchell, "but we'd go on first-class trips to Hawaii with IBM. My dad's adventurism was always a big part of our lives, even when he wasn't on the trip. All our vacations for a decade were his lecture tours."

Fifteen years had passed since Mary Ann and Norman had promised each other they would sail around the world, no matter what. The Heyerdahl expeditions had set back their plans, but Norman was finally home with no more interruptions in sight. It was time to turn their gaze toward circumnavigation.

HURRICANE AGNES

Year: 1972
Category: 1
Highest Sustained Wind: 85 mph

MY SECOND HURRICANE was the year I was thirteen.
Hurricane Agnes began life off the coast of Mexico on June 14, 1972, the offspring of a polar front and a trough over the Yucatán Peninsula.

At just that time, I was finishing seventh grade, my first year at Bullis Prep, the private boys' school where my brother was a year ahead of me. It was an auspicious year for me and—by extension—my family. Academically, I was at the top of my class. I played football, soccer, and track. I was elected class president. And I was miserable. I hated the casual cruelty that seemed to define life at the school, for both students and faculty (who were all male). Bullying was rampant, and asserting one's place in the masculine hierarchy was simply a matter of survival.

At the end of the school year I was called into the main office and informed that I would be the recipient of that year's Headmaster's Award, a prize given for overall excellence in academics, athletics, and citizenship. To all appearances, it was the culmination of a year's hard work. My family was enormously proud, and everyone—Mami and Papi, my grandparents, and my brother—would be at the ceremony at the small church near the school. Still, I hated it at Bullis and began to plot my escape and my return to public school.

The day I received my award, Tropical Storm Agnes was curving northward toward the Straits of Yucatán, a stretch of water between southeastern Mexico and western Cuba. The storm remained off-shore but passed close to Cuba's western tip. On June 18 Agnes achieved hurricane force in the Gulf of Mexico and made landfall the next day near Cape San Blas, Florida, near the convergence of the Florida, Alabama, and Georgia borders. The National Hurricane Center declared it a Category 1 hurricane with sustained winds of seventy-five miles per hour. After a brief stay, Agnes continued inland and weakened as it passed over Georgia and South Carolina, then on to North Carolina, where it made seafall in the Atlantic and got its second wind. Agnes was headed our way.

In those days I had staked out a secret niche in my parents' bed-room. On hot summer days, eager to be alone, I would sneak off to this small haven, a nook near their walk-in closet with a window that looked out on our backyard. It was just the right size, not wide enough for any-thing but lying down. It was a safe, quiet place to lie and read for hours, the sounds of my family reduced to murmurs drifting up from below as I whiled away the afternoons with Salinger's Glass family, Vonnegut's travelers of the space-time continuum, Hesse's Siddhartha. My family felt close, but not too close, and as a result this spot had an almost magical significance for me. I could be alone, but just alone enough.

This day—Tuesday, June 21—I did not bring a book to my nook. Instead, I brought the plaque I had been awarded. It read:

Bullis School
Headmaster's Award
Presented to Nelson Simon
For Leadership in Academics,
Athletics and Citizenship Combined
June 17, 1972

Laying the plaque on the floor by my side, I knelt at the window and gazed out. I saw our backyard, a flat, empty expanse of grass that served as a field for both football and British bulldog, the tackling game that dispensed with the pretext of a ball. Beyond the border of the yard was a steep hill that dropped down to the ravine that ran the length of our neighborhood, and beyond.

Parents in our neighborhood liked the ravine because it ensured that no houses would be built on the back side of their property, thus enhancing the value of their investment. We kids loved it because it brought a certain wildness to the neighborhood, practically to our doorstep. In the center of the ravine was a creek that in quiet times (which was most of them) meandered gently into the woods, its water so low that with a good running start you could scamper across and suffer little more than wet soles. Of course, I knew that today would not be a quiet time, and as I watched, I waited for the transformation. I had seen it a couple of times before when heavy rains had gorged the creek with water that filled the ravine, topping out almost halfway up our hill. Once, Rob and a couple of other older boys had waded into the torrent to pull out three-year-old Georgie Banning, who before the storm had somehow made his way down to the fort the boys had made in a thicket by the edge of the creek. It was as heroic an act as any of us had ever seen, and it became a part of neighborhood lore, recounted at ball games, cookouts, even into adulthood, whenever any of our gang ran into each other.

Inside our climate-controlled house, I couldn't feel the dropping air pressure, but I could see its effects out the window. The leaves on the trees down in the ravine stopped fluttering all at once, as if the air had been suctioned away. The vibrant blues, greens, yellows, and browns of a summer day disappeared, replaced by a purple-gray pallor. I felt an almost uncanny anticipation, as if something just outside the window were saying, *Wait, wait, wait for it.* My hands on the sill, I leaned forward, my forehead and nose touching the windowpane as I tried to feel the storm that was just now arriving. I heard the water before I saw it, a thump, then another, then the rat-a-tat of rain falling, hard, on the roof. The wind arrived, and gobs of water smacked against the side of our house, rattling the window and even managing to drive a few drops past it where the casing failed to provide a sufficient seal. I felt the water on my fingers and ran to get a towel in case the moisture increased.

And then I knelt and watched. The water and the wind settled into a rhythm: hard, driving torrents that at times seemed to rattle the very structure of our house, followed by respites, as if the storm were taking a breath before coming at us again. I watched for a long time. I loved the storm, though I didn't know quite what I wanted from it. Certainly it was nothing like the destruction that Shakespeare's Lear—which admittedly I would not read for some time—calls down. I didn't want Agnes to "smite flat the thick rotundity o' the world." But my year at Bullis Prep had been hard, with difficulties I could not share and that I expected to continue to carry alone. Maybe it would have been OK for the winds to blow and crack their cheeks and drench our steeples, to wash away at least some of what I had been through and give me a chance to start again. If I had been a different kind of person, I might have run downstairs and out the basement door that led to the backyard. I might have run to the edge of the hill and looked out over the ravine, opening my arms wide to let the wind and rain drench me. I might even have brought the plaque with me, thrown it below into the rising water. But I didn't.

After moving through Maryland, Agnes carried on, like a drunken reveler staggering from one locale to the next looking for another drink to keep the party going. A day later, late on June 22, it made its final landfall on Long Beach, New York, on Long Island, with winds of sixty-five miles per hour. But it wasn't done. No longer a tropical hurricane, it began a second life as an extratropical storm, feeding on cold arctic air that refueled it and sent it reeling through Pennsylvania; north to Ontario; east to Cape Breton, Nova Scotia; and finally to Iceland, Ireland, and the Hebrides in Scotland, where it was absorbed by a stronger system on July 6, fully three weeks and almost five thousand miles from where it was spawned. Agnes dropped up to a foot of rain on the East Coast, caused $2.1 billion of damage, and killed 128 people, including 19 people in Maryland.

Because of the hurricane's severity, the name Agnes was retired after the storm and will never be used again.

After Agnes, I convinced my parents to let me go back to public school. In early September 1972 my family was glued to the TV watching the harrowing hostage situation unfold at the Olympics. A group called Black September held members of the Israeli team for most of a day before a showdown with the German military at a nearby airport. We were shaken by the tragic ending—all eleven hostages were killed. Witnessing those sad, shocking events seemed to take the heart out of my hopes for a new beginning.

Days afterward, I began classes at Cabin John Junior High. I lasted four days. On the fifth day I asked my parents to send me back to Bullis. Looking back, it's clear that the issue was never about this school or that school but about the myriad unnamed and unexpressed fears I was grappling with, and that I was doing so alone. I could not tell my parents what was wrong because I didn't know myself. What I did know was that I would have to figure it out on my own. Changing schools was the best that my thirteen-year-old's mind could come up with, but by the end of that first week I had decided to return to the hell I knew. I would remain at Bullis three more years, finally transferring to public school for good in the eleventh grade.

3

ANNE KRISTINE

"It was clear to all of us . . . that this was never going to happen. It was clear to everyone except my dad."

—Elizabeth Baker

DAN BAKER WAS LOOKING THROUGH ME. At least, that's how it felt. I had met Norman's oldest child just a few minutes before, having driven up to the University of Vermont, where he is an associate professor. We sat in his office in Morrill Hall, its neoclassical buff-brick facade a warm beige against the white of the February snow that surrounded it. I had asked him exactly one question, but it was, apparently, the wrong one. I wanted to know about the agreement that Dan and his siblings had signed with their parents, making a commitment to sail around the world as a family. Both his sister, Elizabeth, and younger brother, Mitchell, had mentioned the agreement almost in passing, as a piece of family lore.

One day in 1973 the three kids, led by Dan, then twelve, cornered their father in the kitchen, pulled him into a chair and demanded that he promise that the family would sail around the world. In a playful mood, Norman waffled and tried to weasel his way out of it, but they wouldn't let him up until he put it in writing. After Norman had finished, Mitchell, age nine, wrote, "No backs," a stipulation that no one could back out, and Elizabeth, age ten, added the family pets: Sandy, Taffy, Puss, and Yum Yum. The contract was framed and hung for years in a downstairs bathroom in the family home, both as a reminder of the shared family dream and also, undeniably, as one of those examples of children's seriousness that adults find so cute.

Dan seemed stunned by my question, as if by way of an icebreaker I had casually tossed out, *Tell me about the most painful disappointment of your adolescent years.*

"So, your first question is . . . it's a little bit . . . it's pointed for me," he said with some effort. "I don't really know how the rest of my family saw that agreement, but it was pretty much driven by me. Because since I had been a little baby, my dad had talked about sailing around the world. I really wanted to sail around the world. Didn't want to be in junior high school. Didn't want to be stuck in the suburbs. And I was impatient for us to go." For Dan the contract was a way to make tangible a promise that had been expressed long ago, that for him felt almost genetic in its origins. "Sailing around the world," he remembered, "was present in my mind since I was . . . I can't say since I was born, but it was early. Very, very early."

Indeed, Dan had been trying to get out of town since well before signing anything. Shortly before Norman left for *Ra II* in 1970, the eight-year-old wrote a letter to Thor Heyerdahl and made his pitch for being taken along, pointing out that it would be handy to have a crew member who could fit into spaces where others couldn't go. It was another instance that most likely seemed humorous to adults, but for Dan was deadly serious. He received a letter of thanks from Heyerdahl's wife along with a book about ships.

Looking back, Dan could better understand how in the adult world one year could become three years, then five years, then ten.

But at the time, a teenager's life in New Rochelle, New York, was more than his adventurous heart could stand, and he just took off. By age fifteen he was hitchhiking all over the eastern United States for long periods of time. He crewed on a racing sailboat. Later he went ice climbing in Peru, became a professional river guide, and began sailing professionally. He went down to the Caribbean and skippered charter boats and worked on wooden boats.

For Elizabeth and Mitchell, the thought of a familial circumnavigation held different connotations than for their brother. The prospect of sailing around the world with her family loomed over Elizabeth's life from an early age. "And I do mean 'loomed,'" she said, "because I didn't really want to do it. I wasn't really a sailor. I didn't really want to be on a ship going around the world." As a young girl she negotiated with her dad. She would go if the boat had curtains on the windows, and Norman promised her curtains, "pink, frilly curtains," if that was what it took to get her on board. Unlike his sister, Mitchell longed to see the far-flung places they would visit, and the idea of sailing there on an old ship appealed to his boyhood sense of adventure, though his wanderlust would eventually take him in a different direction. By age seventeen he had left the house and was living in New York City's East Village.

The years did pass. When he wasn't traveling to lecture on the *Ra* and *Tigris* expeditions, Norman worked in the construction business he'd started with his brother Howard. The family bided their time, improving their financial footing and waiting for the right opportunity. Some did arise. At one point a family friend offered them the use of his ship, a fiberglass ketch, but Norman declined. The vision had grown. By then it had to be a wooden ship, and the adventure had to have a greater purpose. Inspired, perhaps, by his experience with Heyerdahl's reed boat expeditions, Norman sought a more audacious mission. He found it in the *Challenger* expedition. From 1872 to 1876 the HMS *Challenger* had become the first scientific vessel in history.

During that time, it had circumnavigated the globe, covered seventy thousand nautical miles, discovered over four thousand species, and laid the foundation for modern oceanography. Norman wanted to sail the same route, stop in the same places, and gather samples from the same waters to chronicle how the earth had changed in the hundred years since.

Mary Ann found the ship in *Wooden Boat* magazine. It was Mary Ann who found everything the family did, who kept the family safe and happy and whole, even when her husband was away for months at a time during the reed boat expeditions. If Norman was Ulysses, Mary Ann was his Penelope, but with a Jewish mother's sensibility and a New Yorker's sense of humor. She seemed preternaturally suited to the role. She loved the sense of adventure her marriage to Norman brought. And while she missed her husband when he was away, somehow she never resented his absence. During both *Ra* expeditions, when her children were still young, she made sure to take them to visit a ham-radio operator, who would patch their father in so that he could talk to them from the middle of the Atlantic. It was Mary Ann who found the house in New Rochelle—who, when she and Norman were dreaming of the house they would someday build, found that it already existed and said, "This is our home." Now she was looking through the classifieds of the boating magazine, and she came upon an ad for a Norwegian schooner harbored in the British Virgin Islands. "This is our ship," she said.

Norman and Mary Ann traveled to Tortola to see *Anne Kristine*, a gaff topsail schooner carrying a square sail. They liked what they saw. They liked the obvious strength of her scantling, the way she was built. They liked that she was double hulled and fully framed, the size of the frames greater than the space between them. They liked that she had a deep keel and a beautifully shaped hull, efficient yet capable of taking high seas. It was clear that she was an eminently seaworthy ship.

Anne Kristine in Tortola in 1982, before repairs began. Photo by Norman Baker

Beyond her physical attributes, they liked her pedigree. *Anne Kristine* was the sister ship of *Gjøa*, the first vessel to transit the Northwest Passage in 1906. After traversing the passage, *Gjøa*'s captain Roald Amundsen had sailed her from Alaska to San Francisco, where the hoopla around the ship's arrival provided a respite as the city recovered from its recent earthquake. Members of the Norwegian American community prevailed on Amundsen to sell them the ship, and she sat, and deteriorated, in Golden Gate Park until 1972, when *Gjøa* finally returned to Norway to be displayed in a museum. By then she was so rotten that when she arrived in Oslo, she fell apart and had to be largely rebuilt. Only 5 percent of the restored *Gjøa*—the keel and a few frames—was original. By contrast, *Anne Kristine* was 60 or 70 percent original.

Finally, the Bakers liked that *Anne Kristine* was Norwegian and had been built only a few miles from where Thor Heyerdahl had been born. It did indeed seem that they had found their ship.

Before finalizing the purchase, Norman hired a professional marine surveyor to inspect *Anne Kristine*. The man was also a marine archaeologist who had worked with ancient ships, often raising sunken ships to examine them. Now he stood before an actual functioning vessel that was built in 1868, the oldest ship in continuous service in the world. The ship was not in the water but sat on ways, a series of large wooden blocks that are used to support a ship when it is in dry dock. The owner had removed the scaffolding around the ship, so the only way to reach the deck was by a series of rickety ladders. The surveyor, an elderly man, was unable to climb to topside, but the ship seemed well maintained. After all, she glistened in the sun, the reflection of the white stanchions visible in the glossy paint of the green covering boards. Granted, he did find small areas of rot, but this was normal on a ship this old, and he noted in his report each thing that needed replacing or repair.

As was the custom, the surveyor also spoke with the shipwright about what work had been done on the ship and what work was still needed. In this case the shipwright was *Anne Kristine*'s owner, and he told the surveyor the same thing he had told the Bakers, that the ship could be ready to sail in three months. The surveyor agreed, the deal was done, and Norman and Mary Ann had bought themselves a ship.

It was 1982, and everything was coming together. Heyerdahl was planning a trip to the Maldives, and he had asked Norman and family to join him as the base ship on that expedition, a waypoint on their voyage. The ship would carry the Explorers Club flag, marking it as an official Explorers Club expedition. They would make a film. Norman would write a book. He would lecture. All of this would make it possible to buy *Anne Kristine* and outfit her, and make it feasible for everyone to stop what they were doing and take two years to sail around the world.

It was time to honor the agreement.

Anne Kristine's previous owner had told Norman that, with a skilled shipwright guiding them, he and Dan, both experienced carpenters, could have the ship ready to sail in a few months. So Norman engaged two young shipwrights, recent graduates, to help prepare *Anne Kristine* for the trip. With their help, Norman and Dan began to attack the parts of the ship that had been left exposed and were clearly rotten. The idea was to dig out the rot, cut back to sound wood and rebuild from there. They began, taking out sections of wood the consistency of ripe papaya, digging and digging as they searched for sound wood hard enough to work with. But they never found it. Again and again, they dug until they saw daylight on the other side. The below-deck accommodations were rotten because the deck had been leaking water into them. The topside planking was rotten because it had not been properly sloshed with salt water, which would have preserved it in the tropics. Hull frames and ribs were rotten. In short, the entire ship was rotten.

After four months they were still ripping out and hadn't even started the rebuild. The shipwrights were disheartened; one of them left because he hadn't been hired as a garbageman, he said. Norman and Mary Ann thought of abandoning the ship, cutting their losses, perhaps looking for another ship. Thus began a process that would occur again and again during the course of the rebuild. It was equal parts assessment, negotiation, agonizing, and just enough self-deception to help them carry on. How deep in were they? How much had they sunk into the project, not simply in cash but in sweat equity and emotional investment? Could they still finish in time to join Thor Heyerdahl in the Maldives?

Because the original owner had so misrepresented the condition of the ship, the Bakers took him to arbitration and won, canceling the balance of the ship's mortgage. They got a price from the shipyard in Tortola to replace the ship's rotted topside planks and to sister the rotted hull frames. Sistering meant they wouldn't take these ribs out;

rather, they would cut away the worst of the rot and put preservative on what remained to keep the rot from spreading. They would then attach "sister" frames to the originals to bring the ship's hull back to her original lines and replace any strength that had been lost. Most of the ship's frames were compromised and would need a sister—forty-five in all. With the canceled mortgage, the Bakers had just enough cash to get *Anne Kristine* seaworthy. Norman's estimate: they were three months away from shoving off.

It was now the summer of 1983, and Norman and Dan had been working on the ship on and off for the better part of a year. Mary Ann and Elizabeth, who had gotten permission to do her senior year at sea for college credit, packed up the house and bought two years' worth of provisions for the circumnavigation. Dan and Mitchell met them, and together they flew to meet their father and begin the family's great, long-awaited adventure. Completing the crew were Dan's dog, Lucy, and the family's eighteen-year-old cat, Taffy, the lone surviving pet named in the original agreement.

Perhaps inspired by the success of the Oscar-nominated documentary *The Ra Expeditions*, which charted Heyerdahl's voyages, the Bakers resolved to chronicle each step of their own adventure. Grainy footage shows the family boarding a small plane in Puerto Rico to fly down to Tortola to meet Norman and finish readying *Anne Kristine* for the voyage. In voice-over Mary Ann asserts that on the way to the airport in New York she had mailed the last payment on their home's twenty-year mortgage. "I began to feel a sense of freedom," she says. "No mortgage and a two-year leave of absence from my teaching job." A shot from the plane's window shows Tortola Harbor. A masted vessel sits not in the water but just at the edge of it, as if someone had dragged the boat ashore. Mary Ann says, "Norman told us there was work to do to get her ready, but she looked good from up here."

The documentary is an odd piece of work. Soundless but for the voice-over, it looks almost like a home movie, but one from a *really* interesting family. Mary Ann and Norman take turns narrating in a folksy, guileless manner. "Oh my," says Mary Ann upon getting a closer look at the ship, "I'd been aboard the previous year when we first saw her, before Norman and Dan began to ready her for the voyage. What had they been doing?" Mary Ann may have already seen the ship when they had first purchased her, but this would be Elizabeth and Mitchell's first look.

The most affecting sequence of the film comes when first Mitchell then Elizabeth climb the rickety ladder that leads to the deck. Shot along the hull of the ship, with the harbor in the background and a tarp hanging into the frame from above, the ship and the tarp form an inverted V into which the younger Bakers seem to disappear as they ascend to the deck. Cut to a shot within the cabin space, as each descends from a rhombus of overexposed sunlight to the darkness of the main saloon below. It is hard to believe the moment is not staged, what with the logistics of repositioning the camera to capture the two shots in the sequence. But there's no denying the authentic emotion on their faces. They look distraught. The camera follows them for a long time as they go over each dark, dank corner of the space. If they're looking for something to feel hopeful about, they don't seem to find it. In a final shot they both look back over their shoulders toward the hatch, Mitchell closer to the camera, Elizabeth in the shadows behind him. Perhaps they are turning because Mary Ann has said something. But they look as if they're hoping someone will come rescue them. Or wake them up.

As upsetting as this moment of discovery was for the two younger siblings, it was not entirely surprising. "My father always underestimated how long something would take. Always, always," Mitchell later told me. "Our house in New Rochelle was always under construction, until the day we sold it." *Anne Kristine* would be no different. She was always 95 percent finished, always three months from launching.

"Of course, it was clear to all of us, and everyone in Tortola, that this was never going to happen," remembered Elizabeth. "It was clear to everyone except my dad."

The work continued. The family hired experienced shipwrights from the shipyard to help them with the tasks that required skilled hands. These were the men who put in the forty-five sister frames to reinforce the ship's damaged frames. Once those were laid in, the workers began to replank. Because *Anne Kristine* was a double-hulled ship, this meant drilling holes through the outer planking, the frames, and the inner planking. Once the planks were bolted in place, they were tarred, ram-caulked with oakum, and tarred again. This made the ship's hull watertight.

While Norman and Dan worked with the shipwrights, the rest of the family dug in, literally, to the less glamorous aspects of the project. A typical day was getting up with the sun, trudging down the hill from the lodgings they had rented, and "scraping a hundred years of shit out of the bilge," as Mitchell put it. They dug out tar and rope from between the teak deck planks. They used solvents. They wore masks. They labored in one-hundred-degree heat and high humidity while being hounded by mosquitoes. "It was messy, filthy work," Mitchell said.

As bad as it was, their life on the island wasn't all just dirty work. Tortola was beautiful. Mitchell and Elizabeth made friends. They visited other tall ships in the harbor. Sometimes they would sneak into parties a local cruise ship threw on the beach. They would clean up the best they could and put on their best clothes, then take the Zodiac across the harbor, and cut the engine just out of sight of the shore. Mitchell became adept at the limbo and often won first prize: a hundred dollars and a magnum of champagne. They lived it up on lobster tail and filet mignon until the fourth time, when the cruise crew finally recognized them and kicked them out. Mostly, though, they just tried to get through each day.

Closer examination of *Anne Kristine* revealed how badly the ship was damaged. Much of the hull had to be repaired or replaced. Photo by Norman Baker

Dan wasn't thrown by the ship's condition or by the prospect of a longer-than-expected rebuild. He had spent a good deal of time in the Caribbean already, working on other ships, and he liked the life. He tried to convince his father that the family should settle down on the islands, work on the ship at a more leisurely pace and extend the horizon of their trip further into the future. (Norman never bought into his eldest son's plan. He worked at a breakneck speed throughout the project.)

Elizabeth and Mitchell, on the other hand, were mostly miserable. Mitchell hated leaving his friends in the East Village and longed to be back in the city's bustle. Once Elizabeth had resigned herself to the trip, she certainly didn't want it stretching out more than absolutely necessary. As it was, she had gotten special permission to spend her senior year circling the globe. She was supposed to be conducting marine biology experiments, collecting plankton samples and analyzing them at each stop along the way. Instead, her professor asked her to study the plankton in Tortola's harbor. Each night Elizabeth took out the family's dinghy and did a plankton tow, took the samples back to the apartment, and examined them under a microscope. She photographed and drew them. Then, loath to harm any living creature, she would take the dinghy out again and release the plankton where she had found it.

Amid all this drama was Mary Ann. Like the eye of the familial storm, she afforded those closest to her a circle of calm, even as the family's situation became more chaotic and unsure with each passing day. Cook, counselor, and common laborer, she kept the family fed, had heart-to-hearts with Elizabeth on long walks after dinner, and did every task that was asked of her and more. And what a worker! This New York City native seemed born to the ship life. In the family's documentary she is there at every turn, doing the dirtiest, most menial jobs with an unwavering cheerfulness. She seems happy to laugh at herself, as when she admits that she and the family dog are the only two afraid to cross the narrow plank to board the ship; when she's nearly finished wiping up the filth from the bilge but knocks over the can where she's collected it; or when she traps herself into yet another corner when painting the deck. She swore a vendetta against the huge Caribbean roaches that infested the ship and spent much of her time meticulously removing them until the ship was free of vermin. Through it all she managed to provide a balance between the rock that was her driven, often quixotic husband and the hard place where her two unhappy younger children dwelled.

Once the sister frames and the topside planking were finished, and *Anne Kristine* was back in the water, Norman hoped that the bulk of the work was over. But the more they did, the more they found. The breast hook was rotten. The transom beam was rotten. The transom knees, samson posts, and mast partners all were rotten. Each of these parts, so logically yet oddly named, so particular and specific in its function, makes up the mysterious, esoteric whole that is a tall ship. For the Bakers, the cruel joke was that none of these jigsaw puzzle pieces had survived the poor care of previous owners. Each one had to be replaced, most of them from scratch.

Norman had acquired a copy of the plans for the *Gjøa*, *Anne Kristine*'s sister ship. Using these, the shipwrights the Bakers had hired fashioned each of the replacement pieces by hand, using traditional tools. For the breast hook, a single V-shaped piece that sat at the bow of the ship and held its two sides together, Norman ventured into the jungle with two local shipwrights. Armed with saws, axes, and a template, they found a tree with a trunk that forked at just the right angle. The transom beam, which supported the stern section of the flat-ended ship, was whittled from the salvaged mast of a ship destroyed in a hurricane. Each replacement was painstaking and painful, using time and money the family had not counted on spending.

Then, Dan gave his father the worst news. Every one of the ship's spars was unsound: the mainmast and foremasts, each consisting of a lower mast and topmast; the main boom and forebooms, the horizontal poles extending from the bottom of the masts; the main and fore gaffs, used to raise and lower the sails; and the bowsprit and jib boom, the two poles that jutted out from the bow of the ship. These ten poles, some of them massive, all had to be replaced. Norman traveled to nearby islands—St. Croix, Puerto Rico, the Dominican Republic. None had timbers the right size. Months went by. Finally, Norman heard that a company in Florida had some beautiful Douglas firs from Oregon lying around. The company's contract to erect power lines had been canceled, and they were looking to sell the wood at a discount.

Norman went to Florida. The poles were perfect: eighty feet long, straight. They had been preserved with pentachlorophenol, or penta, to keep them from rotting. The poles were too long for a container ship, which couldn't handle anything over forty feet, but the captain of a cargo vessel agreed to lash them to his deck. He delivered them to St. Thomas, the only place Norman could find with a crane tall enough to hoist them onto the ship.

First, the penta had to be removed. The sparmaker the family hired insisted that he and his assistant didn't need any protection from the toxic preservative. They lasted four days. The Bakers would have to do the work themselves. Norman fired up *Anne Kristine*'s engine and the ship made the twenty-five-mile trip. The 125-horsepower Wichmann engine sputtered and coughed the whole way, but it got them there. It was a small milestone—the ship's first outing with the family aboard.

The family and their crew proceeded to scrape down the poles while wearing protective gear: disposable white suits, face masks, and goggles. They looked like an ad hoc hazmat team. Once they had taken off the two inches of wood the penta had saturated, they were able to safely start shaping the new spars, following a sparmaking manual Norman had purchased. "I'd never in my life made a spar," he said. Finally, the crane they had hired lifted each pole and gingerly lowered it into place on *Anne Kristine*, guided by Dan and his helpers. She was beginning to look like an actual sailing vessel.

There were other triumphs. Early on, Dan had discovered that the ship's water tank was rusted and leaking. Norman had two stainless steel tanks with total capacity of a thousand gallons made in the States and shipped on the same container vessel that brought their supplies for the circumnavigation. He designed them to be lowered into the hold, with an inch of clearance. Working as a team, the Bakers hoisted the tanks and eased them through the hatch opening. They fit perfectly. Later, Elizabeth and Norman worked together on the steering station. They meticulously designed, cut, and fit all the pieces of the helmsman's bench to create a piece both functional and beautiful. All along, the family tried to balance the quality of their work with the need to finish. Mary Ann constantly reminded Norman, "Completion, not perfection," until the phrase became almost a mantra between them. Sometimes Norman would answer, "It's not perfection; it's just what *Anne Kristine* deserves."

Time passed, and completion kept receding into the distance. Even Norman could no longer maintain the illusion of being 95 percent done and three months from departure. They weren't going around the world. They were two years into this thing, and they weren't going anywhere, not anytime soon. Mitchell was the first to leave, first to St. Thomas, then back to New York to continue his art studies. Elizabeth went back for her college graduation, having completed her senior year studies during the rebuild. She moved to Burlington, Vermont, where she worked in a restaurant. Both she and Mitchell felt lost. As unhappy as they had been for much of their time in Tortola, the circumnavigation had somehow defined them since childhood. It had been the goal toward which the arc of their lives had bent. Was it gone now? Should they set about figuring out the rest of their lives? Their parents continued working on the ship alone, with help from Dan when he wasn't working as a river guide or painting barns. The trip continued to loom over their lives. The call to come back to the island could come at any time.

It was fall 1984, more than two years after Mary Ann had found *Anne Kristine*. She and Norman missed their children, but letting them go seemed the right thing to do. If the family's dream had become a folly, at least it was their own. With much of the heaviest work done, Mary Ann and Norman fell into a rhythm. Mary Ann spent her days poking around with an ice pick "that seemed permanently attached to my hand," she said. When she found a rotten spot, she would dig it out until she found sound wood. Then Norman would put in a dutchman, one or more pieces of good wood cut to fill the space exactly. They lived on the boat with no kitchen or bathroom, eating fruits, salads, and whatever other cold dishes Mary Ann could concoct without a stove. They worked seven days a week, dawn to dusk, diving off the ship into the water to wash off that day's grime. They had spent most of the money they had earmarked for the circumnavigation.

November 1984. The hurricane came suddenly, without warning. *Anne Kristine* was anchored in Tortola Harbor at Soper's Hole, the west end of the island. Hills rose to the north and the south with an opening to the east. This was bad—in the northern hemisphere a hurricane will spin counterclockwise, its heaviest winds blowing from east to west. They were exposed. The ship began to yaw, her bow and stern sweeping left and right around a vertical axis. This was not uncommon, and Norman was confident that their anchor and cables would hold up. After all, *Anne Kristine* had three anchors, one of them a twelve-hundred pounder, the heaviest in the harbor. "And then, all of a sudden, we yawed to the right," Norman remembered, "and we didn't stop yawing. We just kept going." Mary Ann was behind him on the deck. "Where are they all going?" she shouted. The other boats in the harbor were passing *Anne Kristine*. Norman roared, "Mary Ann, they're not going anywhere. We are!" The ship had been torn loose and was being dragged out of the harbor, toward an island called Little Thatch. If they reached it, the storm's ninety-mile-per-hour winds would smash the ship against the shore.

Norman struggled to start the ship's old Wichmann diesel engine. The electric air compressor needed for a start was out for repairs. The only thing on board that could compress air was a diving compressor for the scuba tanks. The gasoline-powered diving compressor could generate three thousand pounds of pressure; the engine tank required five hundred pounds of pressure to start the engine. Norman recalled, "I tried to run the compressor on the deck, but the rain kept drowning her out. So we had to carry the compressor down below to generate air." Once they started the diving compressor below deck, they couldn't stay down there because of the fumes, but they had to monitor the pressure. If it exceeded the five hundred pounds of pressure the engine tank could take, the tank could explode. Norman would hold his breath, check the gauges, go topside, get some air, take another breath, then go back down to check the gauges again. Meanwhile, they were being dragged out of the harbor as bedlam continued all around them. Ships were torn out of the harbor. Trees were blown horizontally. Metal siding was ripped from the huts that lined the shore. It sliced through the air like rippled sheets of aluminum foil. Power transformers affixed to telephone poles along the shore were lashed by waves of water. They exploded sequentially, bursting one after another with an enormous shower of sparks and flame.

Norman looked up and saw that *Anne Kristine* was being dragged past another ship, *Tor Helga*, which was holding steady despite the high winds. Salvation, Norman thought. *Tor Helga* had three anchors out. If he could get to this vessel with a line, its crew could tie it off and hold *Anne Kristine* until he got the engine started. Mary Ann begged him not to go, but he pushed past her. Grabbing the hawser, the thick rope used to moor the ship, he led it through the chocks and jumped in the inflatable Zodiac, just as Mary Ann strapped a life jacket onto him. He started the engine and pulled away, then suddenly remembered the compressor. He called back to Mary Ann to continue to check it, to make sure the pressure didn't build to a dangerous level. He got no reply.

Norman managed to get over to *Tor Helga* at her bow when her owners, a man and woman, called to him from the afterdeck, "Over here! Over here!" The ship had no deck that went alongside—her cabin ran the length of her hull. "So I had to just slip my way back alongside her," Norman said, "holding on to her rivets and every little scrap of her that I could keep my fingers on, but I finally made it back to her afterdeck." Once at the stern, trying to hold the Zodiac steady, he called up to the couple that *Anne Kristine* was dragging, but that he was making compressed air for an engine start, and please could they hold the ship's line just long enough for him to get his engine started.

"We can't," they cried. "We're just barely holding ourselves."

"Run your engine. You're not running your engine. Please hold us just a few minutes. Then you can cast us off."

"We can't. We'll radio for help for you."

He put the hawser in their hands and let go. The Zodiac began to drift astern, its engine beginning to sputter. "We're sorry," they said. And they dropped the hawser in the water. Norman had no choice but to try to get back to *Anne Kristine*. He hoped the compressor had provided enough pressure to turn the engine over. He hoped Mary Ann had been able to keep the pressure from getting too high. And then his engine died. He yanked the cord. It sputtered, ran for a few seconds, and died again. It was dark, and the Zodiac was being driven toward Little Thatch, just ahead of *Anne Kristine*.

Here, again, as he had as a young pilot, as he had on *Circe* and *Ra* and countless other times, Norman exhibited that coolheaded, cold-blooded inability to panic. He methodically diagnosed the situation and broke it down to its discrete elements. Was it a spark plug? The ignition? If that was the case, he was finished. Maybe the fuel wasn't reaching the engine. He began to feel for the gas tank, but he couldn't find it. It had become adrift in the bottom of the Zodiac. Groping in the dark, he pulled it up, found the gas line, found that it had become detached from the engine. It was a simple fix—there were two prongs that had to fit into two holes—except that he couldn't see and the waves made the boat buck like a mad bull and he was being blown toward the rocks off Little Thatch. "And I just couldn't do it," he said. "I would get one prong into one hole and it was too low or I'd get one prong into the other hole and it was too high. I finally got two prongs into two holes and the thing was upside down."

He looked at *Anne Kristine*, saw that she was still dragging, and figured he'd reach Little Thatch just ahead of her. He kept trying to fit the prongs, finally got them, and yanked the cord. The engine started, but by now he was so exposed, far past the lee sides of the hills, that the wind threatened to flip the Zodiac over backward. He put his feet in the bow and pushed everything with any weight up to the bow as well, including the gas tank. He reached back, just able to steer with the tips of his fingers while running the engine just fast enough to keep the boat moving through the water without raising its bow. He managed to get in the wind shadow of *Anne Kristine*'s transom and then back aboard. Mary Ann had indeed shut off the compressor. Norman was able to start the engine, but it ran only a short time before conking out. As the ship was being dragged toward the mouth of the harbor, what was left of its three anchors gained purchase on the mud in the shallows there, slowing the ship, until the main anchor finally grabbed onto some coral, and it held.

The hurricane lasted three days. One hundred and twenty boats were destroyed in Tortola Bay. Norman's hands were shredded from working the ship's cables to try to keep her masts from flying off in the onslaught of wind and water. But the anchors held.

Burning with fever, Norman collapsed into the aft bunk and slept. Not so Mary Ann. She had just experienced her first hurricane, and her excitement trumped her exhaustion. She paced around the cabin, not knowing what to do until she found herself at the small collection of books they had on board. She pulled one down at random, flopped it open, and began to read. She woke Norman and read the passage to him. The book, *Illusions* by Richard Bach, had been a gift from Dan several years earlier. After, the two slept the rest of the day and through the night.

Five days later, they got a letter from Dan, who was living in the state of Washington. He wrote, "With the snappy tortoise pace of the Tortola mail, this will probably reach you after it's all over. But I had a feeling that you two were in a sort of a low." He'd been browsing in a bookstore and had come upon a copy of *Illusions*. He'd opened it and had found a quote he thought his parents would like. It was, of course, the same quote Mary Ann had come upon: "There's no such thing as a problem without a gift for you in its hands. You seek problems because you need their gifts." He closed, "Hang tight. Love, Dan."

———————

In 1963 the Bakers had bought their home in New Rochelle, the house that Mary Ann had found and recognized as theirs. Over the next twenty years they had raised their three children there, had designed and built an entire additional wing to its structure, and had replaced the house's roof with slate they nailed on themselves, piece by piece. The house had been the family's sanctuary when Norman went away on the reed boat expeditions. It was the house they had expected to come home to after the family's trip around the world. In 1983 Mary Ann had dropped off the last mortgage check on her way to the airport to leave for Tortola. Two years later, by the summer of 1985, *Anne Kristine* hadn't left the waters where they had found her, and the Bakers were out of money. Mary Ann said, "We had to choose between our comfortable home and this old ship. We chose the ship."

The Bakers went home one last time. Mary Ann, Norman, and Elizabeth emptied the house of their belongings and tried to finish up the myriad little repairs they just hadn't gotten to, which hadn't seemed urgent when they thought they'd be back: a piece of molding, a section of baseboard, a handrail. It was OK to leave these things undone in their own house, but it was unacceptable to leave them for the new owners to deal with. The Bakers would leave the house the best that it could be.

The three of them worked through the night, packing and repairing, stopping from time to time to reminisce about this memento or that as they wrapped each item and placed it in a box. Just before dawn, they stood at the fireplace, where they had spent so many

Norman works on *Anne Kristine* with daughter Elizabeth. Photo by Mary Ann Baker

evenings together. It was here that Norman had told his children stories of travel and adventure. Here where the dream of their own adventure had grown. Mary Ann and Elizabeth wept, but Norman could only stand and watch. Later he told me, "I think it is good for the soul to cry. I think it's good to let the dam burst and let the tears flow. For whatever reason, I was unable to."

The Bakers were now committed to *Anne Kristine*. They had nothing else. From the day they bought the ship, Norman had worked as hard and as fast as he could. He had worked seven days a week, getting up before it was light and not stopping until it was too dark to see, and he had asked his family to do the same. Early on he and Mary Ann had thought about cutting their losses, perhaps finding a different ship, but those days were long gone. As Norman put it, "I had committed the family to a course from which I could not retreat and could not turn, a course I couldn't abandon." Even so, it was not what he had envisioned as a boy when he had dreamed of sailing to his heart's delight. He wrote at the time, "The interminable work, the unconscionable expenditure of money, the tearing apart of the family fabric, has soured my love for the sea and for sailing." I asked Norman what gave him the strength to keep going in these moments, when his "just three more months" had come and gone, again and again; when they kept failing; when every aspect of the rebuild and circumnavigation looked like not just a folly but a fiasco. He answered simply, "It seemed the only honorable course."

Mary Ann and Norman used to say that once they started something, they always saw it through to the end. It was one of the qualities that characterized their relationship and allowed them to get through so many difficult times. Now, it seemed to be the one thing that kept them going. Like two tanned Zen masters, they lived in the moment. They tried not to think, but simply do, simply be. With the ship, with the sky, with the task at hand. One task led to the next, one day to the next. They did not look ahead, but rather kept their heads down and kept working. Mary Ann had learned how to parcel and serve, the slow, messy process used to protect each cable that would go on the ship by first applying a coat of tar, wrapping it with cloth, and finally winding it with marlin. The tool she used, the mallet, advanced the marlin one-eighth inch with every turn. It took her weeks to finish, and she joked that by the end she understood what it meant to be an "old tar" because she was covered in it.

Norman, with help from island shipwrights, put up the ratlines, the wooden ladders that made it possible to climb up the masts without being hoisted. They sanded, shaped, and fit the cap rails and pinrails, which fit together in an almost dovetail construction. They finished bolting the ironwork to the rails and masts. To do this, Norman found old ironwork manuals and consulted the plans for *Gjøa*. Some of the ironwork they found stored in the bilge; the

Mitchell near the start of the rebuild. He was the first of the Baker children to leave Tortola. Photo by Norman Baker

rest was forged by local blacksmiths. They rigged the booms and gaffs—the spars used to raise and lower the sails—not with a modern crane, but with the traditional block and tackle they would later use to raise the sails themselves. Mary Ann and Norman lost themselves in the work.

And then suddenly, miraculously, they were done. At some point Mary Ann laid the last stroke of varnish on a railing; Norman fitted the last screw on the compass cover. They looked around and found nothing left to fix, nothing left to paint. No rotted wood that needed replacing with a dutchman. No spar or rib or plank or beam that was not sound. All that they could see—and what they couldn't see, they felt—were parts of themselves, of their kids, of the island men they had hired, men who, after the Bakers could no longer pay, insisted on working for nothing because *Anne Kristine* was theirs now and they were going to see her through. One of them, Jim Smith, had told Norman that someday one of Norman's sons would lift up one of Jim's, and they would be even. Jim's brothers, Dolf and Owen, were the men who had ventured into the jungle with Norman in search of wood for the breast hook. Now, Norman and Mary Ann saw the breast hook Dolf had fashioned by hand, using only an adze to carve it. They saw the work of Stuart Bowen, the foreman of the local shipyard, who had so expertly replaced the ship's planks, and of Dave Hagen, the young shipwright from Maine who had created the mast partners, a complex construction of timbers that nestled each mast in place and served to protect the vessel should the mast break off in a storm. They saw the twenty-eight steel eye splices the riggers Lenny and Lorenzo had made for the fourteen shrouds that held up the masts. They saw the labor, and felt the presence, of so many others—sometimes friends, but just as often strangers—who had come aboard to help over the years, drawn by the irresistible energy of the family and the allure of being part of something great.

After three years, thousands of hours, and all their money, it was time to honor the agreement, again.

They bent on the sails, which meant fastening the sails to the yards, and they invited their island friends to come help and to celebrate with them. The Smith brothers came, Jim being the best bender of sails in the harbor. Gloria and Arthur Kimberly came, the owners of the brigantine *Romance*. As a gift they gave the Bakers oil bags, saying that the bags had saved them in the last hurricane and might help *Anne Kristine* weather the next big storm. The Bakers learned that they had been the subject of wagers over the years. Smart money said they would never finish, and a side bet gave odds that their marriage wouldn't survive, either. Mary Ann figured the islanders showing up to wish them well were the happy winners who had played the long odds.

Norman and Mary Ann summoned their children back to Tortola. They loaded their provisions, checked their papers, and finished a few final preparations. On February 19, 1986, they set off to the west under engine power, embarking on what was to be a two-year, seventy-thousand-mile circumnavigation. They made it sixteen miles. Off the coast of St. Thomas, the main bearing of the Wichmann engine burned out, and they could go no farther. Norman called the Wichmann factory in Norway and was told that they did not make those bearings anymore. They looked through the discarded engines in their yard; they didn't have that model. They suggested Norman have the bearing made in Florida, where there were good machine shops. Norman contacted one of those shops and ordered a bearing, but it didn't fit. Norman sent it back. They made another bearing but packed it so badly that when it arrived, one half of the bearing had scoured the other half and ruined it. He sent that one back. Finally, they made a third bearing and it almost fit. But with no funds left to pay a local machine shop, Norman was forced to hand-lathe it himself. By now four months had passed. The family had drained their funds. And Norman, as determined, stubborn, and obstinate as he was, decided he could ask no more of his family. They were done.

An invitation arrived. It was 1986, the one hundredth anniversary of the Statue of Liberty, and *Anne Kristine* was invited to participate in Op Sail '86, the largest modern flotilla of tall ships ever assembled. His family felt it would be a reward for all their efforts, but for Norman it felt like a defeat. Instead of sailing west, crossing every meridian around the world and returning from the east, they had gotten nowhere. They would arrive from the south, having traveled just 1,600 miles. But the family convinced him, and *Anne Kristine* took part, the oldest ship by twenty-five years. Dan considered it one of the best sails of his life—eleven days in glorious weather. For Mitchell one of the best parts of the trip was lying in his bunk, with his head against a port-side plank: "And if we were tacking to the port side, I could hear the rushing water. I could feel the ocean rushing by."

They reached New York Harbor a few days before the Fourth of July celebration. Norman was hoping to get bookings for the big sail, but Mary Ann disagreed. "We don't want strangers on board," she said. "We want to see our friends." She started calling all the friends she could conjure up, most of whom they hadn't seen since leaving for Tortola. The sail was a revelation for Norman. After four years at close quarters, he couldn't really see the ship, couldn't fully appreciate what his family had accomplished. But their friends could. Those seeing her for the first time marveled at this beautiful schooner, while those who had visited the Bakers in Tortola looked around in disbelief at what that derelict hulk had become. *Anne Kristine* was magnificent. Nothing could make up for not sailing around the world with his family, but Norman did find comfort and some redemption in being welcomed home this way.

Op Sail was a fitting start to *Anne Kristine*'s new life, and the friends who accompanied the Bakers that day were just the first of many who would be drawn aboard over the next five years. Mary Ann and Norman had no money left. They had no home except the ship beneath their feet. But it was almost as if the ship, which they had saved from her watery grave four years before, now took it upon herself to care for them. Good things began to happen. They were given free dockage for the summer in Nantucket, where Dan was able to work as a carpenter while he lived on the ship with his girlfriend, Melissa. Mary Ann called the South Street Seaport Museum in Manhattan and asked if they would like to have *Anne Kristine* as an exhibit ship. She was older than anything else in the harbor, and they were delighted to have her. The Seaport became *Anne Kristine*'s official home through 1987, and her unofficial home for several years beyond.

The free dockage was helping the Bakers survive, but they still had no income. Norman had hoped to start booking day sails and other outings on the ship, but these never materialized. Now they heard from their Tortola friends Gloria and Arthur Kimberly, who had been invited to run sail training for Canadian sea cadets. The Kimberlys had had enough of going north and didn't want to run the risk of heading back to the Caribbean during hurricane season, so they had declined, but they recommended *Anne Kristine*. For the Bakers, this was a godsend. For the next five seasons, they ran charters for fourteen- to nineteen-year-old sea cadets for the Sea Venture Society of Halifax. They took out fifteen cadets at a time, the best of Canada's sea cadets nationwide.

In Norman's mind this would stand as a golden period, part of the gift that *Anne Kristine* bestowed on him and his family. He had always said that every adventure should have a higher purpose, and what better purpose could there be than teaching sailing to youngsters who loved the sea as much as he did? He loved to tell about the time he sailed with the cadets from Newfoundland to Halifax, Nova Scotia, and ran into a gale that lasted two days. They had the ship buttoned up and were bashing along, tacking into the wind—the hardest course for a sailing ship. It was summer, and down below it was so steamy that fog was practically rising from the timbers. Rivulets of water ran down the inside of the ship and wet the bunks. Everything, and everyone, was wet. It was miserable.

On the second morning of the storm Norman came on deck, and he heard singing. A cadet stood at the wheel in foul weather gear with her hood off, her face and hair soaked by the rain and spray, her red hair streaming aft in the wind. "'Old McDonald Had a Farm' whipping out from this young lady," Norman remembered. "My goodness, I thought, she must be hysterical. I kind of went up alongside to get a look at her eyes." She seemed fine and was steering the ship perfectly well as she sang. Norman asked her how everything was. "Wonderful!" she said. Wonderful? Was the weather wonderful? Oh, yes. She had been so afraid they wouldn't hit hard weather on this voyage. And she so wanted to see what hard weather was like. And she loved it.

"And here she was," said Norman, "steering with the greatest of good cheer into this bashing gale and singing, 'Old Macdonald had a farm, E-I-E-I-O.' It *was* wonderful."

The income from the cadet program, coupled with Norman's lectures and the construction work that continued under the guidance of his brother Howard, helped to ease some of their financial worries. After living on the ship for a time, he and Mary Ann bought another house (found by her, of course), this one in western Massachusetts. The allure of *Anne Kristine* continued unabated. Down at South Street Seaport, up in Nova Scotia and everywhere in between, up and down the coast, people would find her. Experienced sailors and those who had been no closer to the sea than a Patrick O'Brien novel. Families. Loners. Friends. Friends told friends about this ship they had come upon at the Seaport, with a black hull and white trim and masts the color of honey. "You just gotta see it," they would say.

Norman reveled in the attention for the ship and drew comfort from the fact that the family's work and sacrifice had finally brought them here. His family, which had seemed so fragile at times, was whole again. But Norman wasn't kidding himself. He had brought them to the precipice, and he would never do that again. His children had moved on, which was as it should be. Released from the promise—and the burden—of the circumnavigation, they were finding new challenges, new relationships, new lives.

Now, Norman could move on, too. Or, in a sense, he could move back to the dream he had never abandoned. After all, there was still a world to see, and now he had the ship that could take him there.

4

PREPARATION

"Epic."

—Damion Sailors

B Y EARLY 1991 Norman and Mary Ann had been sailing *Anne Kristine* for almost five years. It had been a struggle, but they had gained strength from each challenge. When they had gambled everything on the ship, they had gone all in on each other as well, and their bond was stronger than ever. The Canadian sea cadet program had allowed them to keep body and soul together, but it was no longer enough. The Bakers' vision was larger, and Norman's dream— a dream first expressed when he was thirteen years old—had never left him.

Back in the '60s, after he and Mary Ann had decided they would sail around the world, Norman began to study for a master's degree in oceanography. It would link his love of the sea with a profession that might take him there, perhaps with a grant to do ocean research. The reed boat expeditions had interrupted his studies, and he had never gone back to complete them. Now, though he still didn't have the

Mary Ann uses a sander. As the rebuild proceeded, the self-proclaimed city girl rose to every challenge. Photo by Norman Baker

degree, Norman was inspired by his friend Thor Heyerdahl, and by the memory of working with Jack Randall, who had gone on to become the world's preeminent ichthyologist. (In a career that spanned seven decades, Randall named 30 new genera and 834 new species of fish.) Norman wanted to emulate these giants, and the expedition he envisioned was appropriately audacious: Challenger II.

HMS *Challenger*, a three-masted Pearl-class corvette, set sail from Portsmouth, England, in December 1872 and returned four years later with so much information about the earth's oceans that it took two decades to analyze it. The completed scientific findings of the voyage were published in 1895 in a report whose fifty volumes and thirty thousand pages rivaled those of the *Encyclopædia Britannica*. Norman wanted to be the first to return to the 362 oceanographic stations the *Challenger* had visited and measure anew the oceans' temperature, currents, water chemistry, and ocean-floor deposits.

Norman considered the enormity of what he was contemplating. He and his family had given all they had in attempting a circumnavigation, and they had made it all of sixteen miles. He and Mary Ann were finally getting their lives back on an even keel, and they did not have the resources to try again. A scientific circumnavigation of this scale would be enormously expensive. Any attempt would have to come on someone else's dime. Norman's role on the reed boat expeditions had earned him a membership in the prestigious Explorers Club in New York City. Now, he called on the club for help. The president of the club traveled with Norman to the Woods Hole Oceanographic Institution, the largest independent oceanographic research institution in the country. Norman tried not to get his hopes up.

The original *Challenger* was the first vessel to venture into the world's unknown waters. Under the command of Charles W. Thomson, a Scottish natural historian, it had invented modern oceanography. Since then, a multitude of vessels had studied every nautical inch of the earth's seas. There were plenty of oceanographic vessels out there doing lots of research. What purpose would a second voyage serve? "But when we spoke to the chief oceanographer at Woods Hole," Norman remembered, "he was absolutely wild to have this done again."

Shockingly, scientists were still using *Challenger*'s hundred-year-old findings as their base data because they could not get research ships to undertake the sort of survey that Thomson and his team had conducted. There was no funding for it. Instead, oceanographic vessels would go out and skewer an issue—set up a narrow, distinct problem in a specific location and then solve it. That patchwork approach forced researchers to cobble together information as best they could. To get a picture of the conditions in, say, the Tasman Sea between Australia and New Zealand, researchers would have to find a ship that was in those waters at a particular time and look up its data. Then, they would find another vessel in the same part of the ocean at a *different* time and look up its data. They would compare the data, allowing for measurement errors because the two ships were using different instruments. But *Challenger* had sailed around the world with the same instruments and used the data on one basis. And that's what was needed: another sequential sampling of the oceans. Specifically, the Woods Hole official told Norman, they needed samples from the top one millimeter of sediment from the ocean bottoms. That was how much would have accumulated on the seafloor in the century since *Challenger*. "We can't get anybody to fund a survey," the Woods Hole oceanographer explained. "It doesn't sound romantic or dramatic enough. But if you do it, we will help you. And we will help you process the data because we need it."

The support of Woods Hole was a coup for the Bakers, but it was only the beginning. They still had to find the money. Norman and Mary Ann had seen through one enormous undertaking—the rebuild of *Anne Kristine*. Now, they were attempting another—the realization of *Anne Kristine*'s potential—with the same fervor. They established an organization—The Challenger II Expedition—and applied for nonprofit status. This opened a world of new funding possibilities, but it also created a catch-22—in order to attract sponsors for an oceanographic expedition of this scale, they had to show that they were already operating as an oceanographic study vessel, something *Anne Kristine* had never done before. As Norman put it, "We needed oceanographers and ocean researchers aboard to give us the status that would lead to more funding." It was like priming a pump. Land a few choice projects, and that would draw the larger pool of funding they were counting on to pull off the circumnavigation.

That was where the Woods Hole endorsement came in. With that in hand, they were able to book two projects: a charter off Santo Domingo, Dominican Republic, with the Center for Coastal Studies to do research on humpback whales and another with Cornell University for a marine biology seminar. These charters would take *Anne*

Kristine to the Caribbean and pay for her to winter there, leaving her in a good position to begin a circumnavigation.

It was now summer 1991. The charters were set for early '92. *Anne Kristine* would need to be prepared, and there was the storm season to contend with. Sail too soon, and they could run into a hurricane from the south; wait too long, and the Atlantic nor'easters would begin to blow. Norman decided on a two-part solution. *Anne Kristine* would sail to Bermuda at the end of October and lay in there for a few weeks. That way, she would be gone before November, when the North Atlantic storms typically begin, and she could avoid any late-season hurricane activity coming up from farther south in the Caribbean.

Because Norman's responsibilities away from the ship had grown— fundraising, writing, lecturing—it was clear that he would be too busy to sail in October. With that in mind, the Bakers began assembling a crew, beginning with a captain. It was a big decision. Since they had found *Anne Kristine* in Tortola almost ten years before, she had never sailed without Norman at the helm. They selected Joey Gelband. Only twenty-seven, Joey had already amassed an impressive record as a sea- man on both the Pacific and Atlantic, including a stint on the *Te Vega*, the last vessel Norman had served on before leaving the South Pacific.

Joey had first met the Bakers briefly on Tortola when *Te Vega* had docked there. He had been taken by the couple and their audacious project. Joey was a romantic himself. When he was sixteen, he had loaded up his pickup truck with his rottweiler, Bear; a cooking kit; a bag of rice; and some beans. He had driven west from his home in South Carolina with no discernible plan other than to see the Pacific Ocean. He had stopped in New Orleans, then made his way to Colo- rado, where he stayed with a friend of a friend. In Colorado he saw people picking hay, introduced himself, and said, "I've picked a lot of hay. Can I work for you?" (This seemed to be Joey's principal way of finding work, and it would prove surprisingly successful.) From there he drove to the Grand Tetons, across Idaho, and up to La Push, a village on the west coast of the Olympic Peninsula in Washington State. There he saw the Pacific Ocean for the first time. His quest achieved, he wandered down the coast to the fishing docks of Newport, Oregon, and talked himself into a job as a lumper. He unloaded fish for twelve to sixteen hours a day—an inauspicious beginning, but for a young man with a world of confidence and a refusal to take no for an answer, it was entry enough. By his early twenties, Joey had sailed on everything from wooden tall ships to steel-hulled fishing boats to *Edna*, the 135-foot freighter captained by Nancy Griffith, the legendary yachtswoman. He had also worked on cadet training vessels, so when he heard through the "coconut network" that the Bakers were looking for help with the Canadian Sea Cadets, he headed up to Nova Scotia and reintroduced himself to the couple.

In those early days together, Norman and Joey built a bond of mutual respect and even affection. Perhaps Norman saw something of himself in this scrappy kid. Certainly, he admired the young man's grit and his refusal to be put off by rejection, no matter how emphatic. Once, an exasperated skipper—after turning down Joey's request for a job a dozen times—had asked him, "What part of *NO* do you not understand?" Joey had replied, "Not to be disrespectful, but I don't understand the *N* and I don't understand the *O*." He finally got the job, his first on a fishing boat.

The more Norman got to know Joey, the more confidence he had in him. Norman appreciated the level of professionalism and seamanship that his first mate brought to the position, as well as his ability to connect with the teenage cadets. After all, he wasn't much older than they were. Only in his twenties, Joey had already spent almost a decade working on the water, and he approached that work with a single-minded attitude that must have reminded Norman of himself. They did not always agree, but each was willing to listen to the other.

One night, they hit some dangerous weather coming into Halifax with a group of sea cadets. As Joey remembered it, Norman wanted to head right in, but the first mate realized the shoals and current at that spot made a direct approach impossible. Joey recommended they tack out and keep a danger bearing on a light on the shore, using a compass and the fixed light to ensure they were well clear of the shoals. Norman at first agreed, but then, deciding he didn't agree after all, tried to head in directly anyway. But Joey was sure of what he knew. "We would have run aground," he said, "but I finally got through to him." Once near the dock, they managed to get behind some buildings that served as a windbreak. They got their sails down and rode out the storm. Later, when Norman tried to say something, Joey stopped him. "And I said to him," he recalled, "'Norman, it could have been me. We've got two sets of eyes thinking on this thing, and we're here to help each other. And that's my job.'" Their bond was sealed.

After that first season with the cadets, Joey stayed on the ship. He wintered on her in Sheepshead Bay, with Benny Boy, his pit bull. He taught Benny Boy how to climb the Jacob's ladder. Later, the Bakers would take care of Benny Boy when Joey traveled back west.

Joey was between sailing jobs when he got the call. Norman asked if he would come back. *Anne Kristine* was about to embark on a new adventure, and he wanted Joey to be a part of it. This would not be a jaunt to Nova Scotia with some sea cadets. These were charters of a different order—the Caribbean, scientific expeditions—with the promise of more as Norman booked other work. And here was the kicker—Joey would be at the helm. He had never captained a vessel, had only recently qualified for his Ocean Master's License. *Anne Kristine* would be his first command. Norman would meet the ship in Bermuda to continue the journey to the Caribbean, but he would have to return to the States to keep the project moving forward. Joey would remain and run the operation in Norman's place.

In the sailing world Joey inhabited, you always kept a bag packed because you never knew when one job would end and another begin. Job security, steady relationships, stability—these were abstractions that did not apply to you. You were a vagabond. But with Norman's offer, Joey would be a made man. He picked up his bag and headed back east.

Joey arrived in New York in September 1991 with just over a month before departure. He needed to finish preparing *Anne Kristine* while helping the Bakers fill out the rest of the crew. Joey thought first of his friend Damion Sailors. The two had met two years earlier when Joey was assembling a crew for *Edna*, Nancy Griffith's cargo ship. Damion showed up, a cocky seventeen-year-old with exactly no sailing experience, and declared he would be great at this—after all, just look at his surname. Joey laughed and decided to take a chance on the kid. He was eager and not afraid of hard work. It turned out to be a good call. Damion stayed on *Edna* for a year, and Joey came to rely on him. They understood each other. Both came from difficult family situations. Joey's father was a hardened ex-marine who sometimes treated his son like a new recruit; Damion's dad had left the family when he was a just a boy. Both had left home as teenagers in search of lives vastly different from those they had known. Together they sailed all over the South Pacific, hauling cargo between Hawaii and Tonga, the Cook Islands, and French Polynesia. They delivered rice, flour, sugar, building supplies, and even the occasional Toyota truck. It was, as Damion remembered it, "epic."

Damion left *Edna* and went back to Hawaii, but he soon returned to help Nancy Griffith with her next endeavor: adapting a Japanese fishing boat to haul cargo. After several months in Japan, Damion returned to Hawaii again, this time with a Japanese girlfriend. That's when Joey's call came. Damion recalled, "And he's like, 'Hey, man, there's a really cool gig. You know, we're going down to the Caribbean on *Anne Kristine*.' And I was like, 'Wow, man, you know, I got my old lady here. I don't want to leave her high and dry, you know?'" But he did. He just couldn't pass this up.

By now it was early October, and Joey was busy getting *Anne Kristine* ready for the trip. She was still docked at Kingsborough

Community College in Sheepshead Bay, Brooklyn. That was where the prep work began (and where my friend Peter discovered her during his vision quest). Maintaining any vessel is a big job, but keeping a tall ship running is constant work. You start varnishing a rail, and by the time you do the rest of the ship, it's time to sand and varnish that first rail again. With the ship still in the water, Joey, the Bakers, and assorted volunteers began to work on the hull above the waterline. They put down a skiff—a shallow, flat-bottomed boat—next to the ship so that they didn't spill anything in the water. Then, they scraped, varnished, painted. Every inch of *Anne Kristine*, above deck and below, was refreshed and renewed. They tuned the rigging, a complicated, tedious process to ensure that the ship's masts, sails, and lines were all balanced and functioning properly. They took apart every pulley—called blocks—and greased them. They inspected everything and made whatever repairs were needed.

Once *Anne Kristine* was shipshape above the waterline, Joey and Norman pulled away from the dock at Kingsborough Community College and motored her the few miles to Muller's, a boatyard in Mill Basin. The big U-turn took them along the Rockaway Inlet and under the Marine Parkway Bridge, then into Jamaica Bay. Joey steered *Anne Kristine* between Floyd Bennett Field and Ruffle Bar, a small, deserted island whose waters once produced the best oysters and clams in New York City. He guided her into the small opening of Mill Basin, then into the smaller opening of East Mill Basin, the traffic of the Belt Parkway roaring overhead. Arthur Muller, the boatyard's owner, was a German immigrant who built, repaired, and maintained wooden boats and yachts. He brought an old-world sensibility and a craftsman's standards to the work. For older boats, there was no better yard in New York City.

Muller's men hauled *Anne Kristine* out of the water and put her on ways. Then they went to work, scraping or sandblasting the hull to remove barnacles, old caulk, and other buildup, then recaulking between the planks to ensure a thorough seal. Finally, they gave her a bottom paint. When they were done, she looked new. The workers reminded Norman of the men he had worked with on Tortola, old guys keeping a dying art alive. They checked the propeller, checked her through-hull fittings, intakes from the engine—everything. As they worked, the men found other work that needed doing. That was not unusual on an old boat. Norman and Joey sat down with the repairmen's recommendations and assessed the situation. It was October, and they would soon be up against the window for a safe journey. And while the additional fixes were needed, none were critical. The ship was sound. Let's get out of New York before the nor'easters whip up, they reasoned. Once Joey was in Bermuda, he could lay over in the warm weather. Norman would join him, and they could take whatever time was necessary to put the final touches on *Anne Kristine*.

In addition to the repairs, the Bakers installed a brand-new single-sideband radio donated by one of the ship's devoted volunteer crew members.

While the repairs proceeded, the Bakers were scrambling to get an experienced crew together, with little luck. Norman had a list of seasoned volunteers who had sailed with them at one time or another, but no one seemed to be available. Of the regulars, only Peter Abelman would be on the trip. Peter, a general contractor, had worked with the Baker brothers on construction projects, but had dealt mostly with Norman's brother Howard. Peter was an avid amateur sailor, and one day Howard asked if he would like to help Norman bend the sails on his boat. Peter arrived at South Street Seaport expecting a sailboat and found *Anne Kristine* waiting. As he liked to put it, "I stepped onboard and fell in love with an older woman." He became one of the Bakers' dearest friends and one of the ship's greatest champions, sailing with Norman whenever his schedule allowed. He even began studying for his captain's license so that when the time came for the Challenger II circumnavigation, he would be ready to quit his day job and join the expedition. At fifty, Peter was the oldest member of the crew. (I was the next oldest at thirty-two.)

Another experienced hand the Bakers tracked down was Barbara Treyz. Barbara had left her childhood home in Connecticut in the early '80s to study marine zoology in Hawaii. After learning about *Anne Kristine*, she contacted Norman during the initial shakedown cruises off Tortola and asked for work. Norman suggested she first get some sailing experience. In sailing's insular world, that led her to *Edna*, where she sailed with both Joey and Damion. Later, Barbara came back east and contacted Norman again. This time he brought her on as cook for several of the sea cadet charters. Barbara was a good addition to the crew—she knew the ship well, had a good connection with Joey, and was a team player. After Bermuda, she would stay on as ship's cook on the Caribbean charters.

Finally, Norman called a young man from Pittsfield, Massachusetts, named John Nuciforo. His inclusion on the crew seems a clear indication of how far down his list Norman had gotten. When asked about his sailing experience, John could only point to his town's native son, Herman Melville. He said, "He wrote *Moby Dick* looking at Mount Greylock. The white whale was that hump of snow on the mountain." Not much of a qualification, but the wide-eyed twenty-six-year-old had given the Bakers a lot of free labor on the ship, once even bringing a mechanic friend to check *Anne Kristine*'s engine. Joey needed the extra hands, and the trip to Bermuda would be a reward for John. After the arrival, he planned to travel around the islands.

It was already late October when Laingdon Schmitt picked up the phone in the apartment he shared with his girlfriend. It was Norman Baker calling, looking for Sue. She was out, so Norman left the message with Laingdon—leave in a few days, a week or so to Bermuda; from there Sue would need to make her own way home. Laingdon remembered, "I said, 'You know, she's working two jobs right now, one down at South Street Seaport. I don't think she can make it, but

I'll certainly let her know you called.' And Norman said, 'Well, if she knows anyone else who would be interested . . .' I said, 'Oh, well. I would be.' And Norman said, 'Who are you?'" Laingdon explained that he had been sailing since the age of twelve, and that he had crewed on a fifty-three-foot passenger scooter in the Gulf of Maine. He had worked on a small schooner in Penobscot Bay and on the *Clearwater* sloop the year before. Laingdon was in.

To this group the Bakers added Jen Irving, a young professional sailor, as first mate, and Marty Hanks, a professional chef and amateur sailor who had sailed with *Anne Kristine* in the past.

With a crew nearly in place, Norman and Joey rushed to finish all the last-minute preparations and details that come up before the start of any trip. Primary among these was making sure all the pumps on the ship were fit and ready to go, and that the captain knew how to use them. Next to the sails, a ship's pumps are perhaps the most important equipment on board, especially on an older vessel, where taking on some water could be expected. *Anne Kristine* had a full complement: one big hand pump on deck; three small pumps in the bilge, which were used to control normal seepage; and two large centrifugal pumps. In addition, Norman had recently installed a valve that allowed the ship's Cummins diesel engine to draw water from the bilge instead of sucking it from the sea, which was the normal way the cooling water was ingested into this engine.

Norman took Joey below. Peter, who had never seen the pumps working, asked if he could join them, but Norman had other things for him to do. Once in the engine room, Norman opened the sea cock to flood the ship, putting tons of water into *Anne Kristine*'s bilge. He then opened the priming valves. While he explained the valving systems, the suction hoses filled up, and the water level rose to the level of the pump impellers and covered them. After a few minutes, he turned on the pumps, and water exploded out of the pump's three-inch hose as if shot out of a water cannon. Soon, the bilge was empty.

Norman went over how to switch the valve on the engine-cooling pump so that it too could draw water out of the bilge if that became necessary. This was the ship's biggest, most powerful pump. Using bilgewater to cool the engine presented a hazard because water brought up from the ship's bottom would contain debris—dirt, sawdust, whatever. If that water reached the cooling heat exchanger, it would likely clog it and overheat the engine. To prevent this, Norman had fitted mesh screening over the end of the suction hose leading down to the bilge and had stored even finer mesh screens in the engine room. He went over all of this with his captain.

Joey, for his part, told Norman the old on-deck Briggs & Stratton gasoline pump was beyond repair. Sometimes it would run, sometimes not. The pump was replaced just hours before our departure.

Everything was in place.

Dan and Norman; the rebuild tested the very fabric of the Baker family.
Photo by Mary Ann Baker

Ever since he had watched ships disappear beneath the horizon as a boy, Norman Baker had dreamed of being on one of them, of seeing what lay beyond that hump in the distance. He yearned for adventure, but his mentors had taught him that adventure should serve a greater purpose. Now with Challenger II he could have his greatest adventure and marry it to a noble purpose. The original *Challenger* had opened the door to the modern exploration of the sea and had amassed enough information to fill an encyclopedia. *Anne Kristine* would bring the knowledge garnered by that great ship into a new century by going back to the same places to see how they were doing a hundred years later. By doing so, the Challenger II Expedition could lay the foundation for oceanic exploration and discovery into the next century.

This trip was the next step in that endeavor. It would all begin now, with eight experienced sailors . . . and me.

HURRICANE GLORIA

Year: 1985
Category: 4
Highest Sustained Wind: 140 mph

MY THIRD HURRICANE was the year I was twenty-six.
The reports began early on the morning of September 24. A powerful hurricane had passed near the Bahamas and was expected to move north up the US coast. Back in those days—before everyone had instant access to the latest weather data—we didn't hear about every tropical depression that formed in the Caribbean. So when the weather made the news it was best to pay attention.

Hurricane Gloria was a Category 4 storm. That was bad. Anything above Category 3 is considered a major hurricane (the scale only goes up to 5), and officials predicted that damages could be catastrophic. Forecasters expected Gloria to be the worst storm to hit the East

Coast since Agnes in 1972, and the first of any consequence to make it all the way to New York City since Hurricane Donna in 1960. The director of the National Hurricane Center was calling it "the storm of the century."

I hit the snooze button and rolled over.

By fall 1985, I was completing an arc that had begun four years earlier, on the eve of my college graduation. Then, I had sat alone in the Davidson College theater department, staring at a poster of a young man looking up at the stars. It was an inspirational poster. The text of the poster said something lofty and idealistic about reaching for the stars. I did not feel lofty or idealistic. But in that moment I decided I would become an actor—not because of my passion for the theater, though I did dearly love it, but because I had no idea what else to do with myself.

As a child I had imagined a ceremony, a sort of coronation. I pictured myself seated in a high-backed chair, my family—Mami, Papi, Abuela, Abuelo, Rob, and others—seated on either side of me in a V formation. At the appropriate moment, someone—a celebrant I could never quite make out—would place a crown upon my head. In my vision, the crown did not signify status or property or wealth. Rather, it was the crown of knowledge or, more precisely, self-knowledge. This vision promised me that all would be made clear, my purpose and the path forward illuminated, if only could I hunker down and wait. And so I waited. I became an expert at waiting, at doing as little as possible, at playing the long game.

After four years of college, I faced the chasm of the rest of my life without a plan. There was no work I wanted to do—indeed, no work I felt qualified to do. Looking back, I am struck by how alone I felt in making this decision. I did not consult with anyone, nor did it ever occur to me that this would be a useful thing to do. I simply decided. And having decided, I kept the information to myself. My family had traveled to Davidson for my graduation, but I did not tell them about my plans.

I graduated, went home to Maryland, went to Bolivia, came back. My return to Bolivia was my first since I had left at age three. It was my "roots" journey, I said. An opportunity to understand myself by rediscovering the land and people I had come from. I stayed four months, traveling on ancient buses and trains, and in the backs of large trucks filled to bursting with people and produce. I met aunts and uncles and cousins, none of whom I remembered, who treated me, paradoxically, both like a long-lost child and as if I had just left the room. They had been waiting for me. It was as if the passage of time meant nothing to them. Whether I was age three or twenty-two, they would love me just the same. The trip was a revelation to me but did nothing to help me figure out what to do next.

When I got back home, I dipped a toe and then waded fully into the theater. I auditioned for whatever I could find in the DC area, even took an acting class or two. I got my first paid job as an actor at the Court Jester, a dinner theater in Silver Spring, Maryland. In that production I met a woman I was sure was the first *real* actor I had ever known. She had studied. She had a technique. I was in awe. I had never seen anyone work the way she did—with such a sense of purpose and intention. I was smitten, and before my heart broke for the love of her, she managed to point me toward New York City and the Neighborhood Playhouse, the school that Sanford Meisner had built.

Meisner, a colleague of both Lee Strasberg and Stella Adler, had come out of the Group Theatre in the '30s. All three became teachers of acting, each one imbuing the discipline with his or her own beliefs about the actor's craft. Meisner was the least known of the three. A documentary of his work dubbed him "the best-kept secret of the American theater." For me, Meisner and the Playhouse were less a secret than an answer. Finally, I had found a program, a place where I could pour my energies and come out better than I had gone in. It was a rigorous program—two acting classes a day; dance, both ballet and modern, the latter based on the work of Martha Graham, who had taught at the Playhouse in the '20s; movement; singing; voice; and diction. For the first time I realized how important structure was to me. Academic studies had come easily but had never engaged me. Here, I was challenged every day—creatively, emotionally, physically. There were times I felt pushed to the limit of my abilities and comprehension, but I couldn't wait to go back and try again every day. Our first-year acting teacher said to us, "You will take in everything we're saying, and you will do what we ask of you, but there's only so much you can understand right now. Then one day, a year from now, two years from now, you'll be walking down the street and your head will fall off, because you will suddenly *get* it." I loved that kind of talk.

Mami and Papi were scared for me and wondered what to make of me, but they never stopped trying to support me as I struggled to find my way. Years later, during a crisis in my forties, I would finally share some of the doubts and fears I had kept hidden much of my life, but in 1985 that was still a long way off. Now they arranged for me to live with an elderly Nicaraguan lady, a sort of surrogate grandmother I called Doña Adela. She lived in the Jackson Heights neighborhood of Queens with her daughter Lila and her grandson. Having a loving and stable home was just as important as all I was experiencing at the Playhouse. I thrived. And when my Nicaraguan family moved out to Staten Island over the winter break and asked me to move with them, I did.

The move was crucial, though I didn't know it at the time. My short subway commute became a two-hour trek by subway, ferry, and train. The second-semester work at the Playhouse was ramping up, becoming more challenging emotionally and physically. The combination left me exhausted. In May, toward the end of the school year, a classmate asked me if I would like to move into the small one-bedroom he had just rented on the Upper West Side of Manhattan. I said yes.

As we began to rehearse our scenes for the final showcase at the Playhouse, the import of the moment began to hit me. The Playhouse accepted three classes for the first year, about sixty students, but invited back only one-third of those for the second year. For most of the year I had assumed I would get asked back, but in the last months I had lost my confidence and began to feel I had stumbled badly. The scene I was assigned did little to reassure me. It was a lighter comic scene without much emotional range, and I was partnered with a woman I didn't think would make the cut. Not good signs.

The scene went well, and several second-year students gave me the thumbs-up afterward. You're in, they said. You're in for sure. I went back to my tiny, barely furnished room and awaited the letter from the Playhouse.

A week later I opened my mailbox to find the slender envelope that could mean only one thing.

Once I learned I would not be invited back for the second year, the thread that had kept me tethered to a purpose snapped, and part of me floated away. Worse, I had left the love, warmth, and regular meals that Doña Adela and Lila provided. I woke up in the mornings with no class to get to, no schoolwork to be done. I lay in the metal-framed bed that was one of the only pieces of furniture in my room and listened as my radio alarm went off. It was permanently tuned to WCBS, the oldies station. Everything about the station's morning programming comforted me—the incessant banter, the familiar ads, the cheerful songs. I relished the station's familiar rhythm.

My acting studies had gone from a full-time theater program to private classes two evenings a week, so I had a lot of time to fill. What eventually got me out of bed each morning was the day's first deadline: the 10:00 AM cutoff for the breakfast special at the neighborhood diner.

For the round, reasonable sum of two dollars, I could get a modest meal, a couple of coffee refills, and a place to sit long enough to leaf through that day's *New York Times*. What I cared about most was the skimpy sports section. The Mets team of the early '80s had rekindled my interest in baseball.

I put down such minutiae now—morning radio, breakfast, baseball—because, in a life suddenly stripped of purpose and structure, these were the details I clung to. Little by little, I began to find freelance work as an editor and proofreader. I spent time poring over my acting scenes and rehearsing with my classmates. I made as much of a life as I knew how at the time. But when I think back to those days it is these images that come most clearly to mind: of a young man not sure what will come next, hunkered down and filling the time until it does.

In acting class one of my scene partners was named Gail. She was from Ohio and had a warm, guileless manner I found easy to be around, less work than the sharp angles and elbows I got from my New York acquaintances. Gail was a dancer who wanted to act. At thirty-five she could feel the first effects of gravity and time, could see the younger versions of herself showing up at auditions with the same verve and optimism she had felt when she first arrived in the city. It was time to move on. She also wanted to have a child. I avoided asking her how she imagined pulling off two such disparate, all-consuming goals as acting and motherhood at the same time, though it hung in the air each time I saw her. Her fiancé was a classical pianist, a snob who dismissed any music outside the Western canon and dismissed you if you disagreed with him. I was convinced he would never marry Gail, much less have a child with her, and I secretly hoped they would break up so that she could move on from him as well. Occasionally, she would open up to me about her frustrations and doubts about her choices and her guy. I listened dutifully, sharing little about myself in return.

As the end of September approached, we followed Gloria's progress as it moved up the coast. On September 25 the center of the storm was four hundred nautical miles east of Miami, and a hurricane watch was issued from South Carolina to Virginia. The center passed over the Outer Banks of North Carolina early on September 27 and accelerated on a north-northeastward path.

We began to get ready.

Gail and I decided her place would be the perfect venue from which to experience the hurricane. We awaited the storm's arrival as we would have the opening of the latest movie blockbuster. It was *Jaws* or *Star Wars* or *Raiders of the Lost Ark*. And if you missed it, well, you missed it, and you could never get that moment back. I took the train from the Upper West Side to Manhattan Plaza and went up to Gail's place on the thirty-seventh floor. We were well stocked with snacks and drinks. I had brought my toiletries and some shorts in case the storm knocked out the city and I was forced to spend the night on Gail's couch. We taped her windows—big plate-glass windows that faced east toward Times Square—as we had been instructed. We watched footage of the havoc Gloria had wrought on its journey to New York City. We waited as darkness descended on the city.

And then nothing.

Well, not *nothing*. We saw some rain pelting the windows and felt the panes vibrating in the wind. Low clouds swirled not far above us. We watched TV as local on-the-scene reporters—at the East River, at Central Park, even at the Montauk lighthouse at the tip of Long Island—tried and failed to inject some drama into an event that refused to yield any. Even the usual idiots who insisted on defying warnings and going outside to the park or out to Coney Island looked foolish, though not for the usual reason.

Was that all there was? I felt deeply disappointed, almost betrayed, though by what or whom I could not say. We turned off the TV, and I sat with Gail in the deepening shadows. We had turned off most of the lights and lit some emergency candles for added drama. There, in the near-darkness, I began to tell Gail something about my life, more than I ever had—about what had brought me to New York, about my time at the Playhouse, even about what I did every day. We talked late into the night, then went out the next morning to see what the city looked like.

Years later, Hurricane Sandy would be the storm that Gloria was supposed to be. Over the course of forty-eight hours, Sandy would leave forty-four New Yorkers dead; damage or destroy sixty-nine thousand residential units, leaving hundreds of thousands of New Yorkers temporarily displaced; and leave hundreds of thousands more without power while casting the southern third of Manhattan into darkness for over a week.

Sandy would be terrible, and it would bring the city together, give us purpose, and make us feel shocked and saddened and vibrantly alive in its aftermath.

5

DEPARTURE

"Motoring under fore and jumbo [sails]. Swell building, wind still light, clear skies. Prepare storm [sail] for setting."

—*Ernestina's* log

O N OCTOBER 23, 1991, the day of Norman's lecture, the first wisps of what would become Hurricane Grace began to coalesce. A low-pressure system formed high above the water's surface somewhere between Bermuda and the Dominican Republic and slowly worked its way down toward the water. By the afternoon of Friday, October 25, the German ship *Holtsencarrier,* sailing the seas southwest of Bermuda, recorded a ten-knot westerly wind. The low had reached the surface.

Just after midnight on Friday, October 25, precisely twenty-four hours before we motored out of Mill Basin, *Ernestina*, a 156-foot schooner, left New Bedford, Connecticut, also bound for Bermuda. Originally launched out of Gloucester in 1894 as a fishing boat, she was now a teaching vessel. She had thirty-five on board, including eleven instructors and twenty-four trainees—"a good, solid crew,"

Anne Kristine. Photo by Norman Baker

according to Captain Gregg Swanzey. Bermuda was the first stop on a six-month transatlantic voyage to the Azores, Portugal, Cape Verde, Barbados, and back to New Bedford via the Caribbean.

At 3:00 AM *Ernestina* motored through Quicks' Hole, a gap between Nashawena and Naushon, two small islands that look like they tumbled off the southern end of Cape Cod, and proceeded past Martha's Vineyard. It was unseasonably warm. "We were wearing T-shirts," Swanzey recalled. Visibility was good, winds light. Twenty hours later, *Ernestina* was 230 miles due east of Tom's River, New Jersey, and about the same distance from Mill Basin, where *Anne Kristine* was in final preparations before departure. The ship passed into the Gulf Stream in the wee hours of the twenty-sixth, and by 1:30 PM the crew stopped the engine and prepared to do some sail training.

They set the main-, fore-, jumbo, and jib sails and continued sailing a steady course south and east. "At that point we were kind of jubilant," said Swanzey. "We thought it might be an easy trip to

Bermuda. And then it changed." A low-pressure system was deepening to the south. As they set the sails, they also prepared for a developing storm, which they noted in the ship's log:

> Ship both anchors and lash all boxes and gear, batten some hatches, prepare ship for possible wind developing from gale center at 32° N65° W due to move to 34° N66° W at 1200 Monday and out of the waters by Tuesday.

This unnamed gale was a tropical depression southwest of Bermuda. According to the information the crew was receiving—via weather fax, the radio, and Coast Guard reports—the storm was tracking north and west. After two days that would place its center 270 miles northwest of Bermuda and 500 miles due east of Wilmington, North Carolina. Although he was keeping an eye on the developing storm, Swanzey did not alter his course.

The morning of Friday, October 25, I made my way back to Mill Basin, ready to embark on my great adventure. I found my friend Peter waiting on the dock. I was glad to see him, and I appreciated his coming to see me off. I knew how bitterly disappointed he was, how he felt I had somehow usurped his place. After all, this was supposed to be his journey of spiritual enlightenment. I didn't disagree, and as we hugged, I almost whispered to him that I wished we could trade places. But I stopped myself. No one could change anything now, and I felt it would have been a cruel thing to say to my friend. Peter wished me well, made a small joke about not falling in love with some charming Bermuda lady. I laughed and promised to come home even if I did. I walked up the plank and turned one last time to wave; then I stepped on deck.

I took a few tentative steps, looked around, listened. Voices rose from below deck. I had expected the ship to rock, but it was still, like the air around me. It was warm for the end of October and muggy, more like a late summer's day. Not knowing what to do, and not wanting to put a foot wrong in this strange new place, I waited. Joey appeared and came over. He looked like a cross between Popeye and Andy Griffith, an old salt's soul, tempered with a Southern softness that his quiet drawl did nothing to dispel. He greeted me and handed me a collection of what looked like sticks and string. He asked me to do something with it. Was this a test? I was to wrap the string or loop the string or do something with the string. I wasn't sure what he was asking me to do, but I imagined it was something I was supposed to know, so I didn't ask any questions. I would figure it out. After Joey left, I tried to make sense of the contraption in my hands but with no luck. I put the mangled mess somewhere out of sight and hoped it wasn't anything too important. *Oh God*, I thought, *this is going to be a long trip.* I went below to meet the rest of the crew.

I had been told we would be departing Friday morning and had rushed to get to the ship early. But the day wore on, and the bustle of preparation diminished, until it seemed no one was doing anything. We were all waiting. Finally, someone told me why: it was bad luck to set sail on a Friday, so we were waiting until after midnight to depart. How could Friday be bad luck? I asked. It seemed the ideal day to start a trip, what with the weekend ahead. No one seemed to know what made Fridays unlucky. Like so many superstitions, its origin has been long forgotten. (Turns out it's in deference to the crucifixion of Jesus.) Sailors are a superstitious bunch, which is perhaps not surprising for a group whose lives and livelihood depend on the vagaries of so much that is out of their control. They have so many superstitions, in fact, that it seems a minor miracle they make it out of port at all.

Besides Friday departures, wary seafarers also avoid Thursdays (out of respect for Thor, the god of thunder and storms), the first

Monday in April (the day Cain killed his brother, Abel), the second Monday in August (the day Sodom and Gomorrah were destroyed), and December 31 (the day Judas Iscariot hanged himself). Bananas, redheads, and whistling are verboten on board. All bad luck. It's bad luck to shoot an albatross. Seabirds are said to carry the souls of departed seamen, so it is a good omen to see one but bad luck to kill one. The right tattoo can help. Tattoos have long been part of sailor culture, because sailors believed that certain images carry great power. For example, seafarers often got a tattoo of a nautical star or compass rose because they believed these could help guide them home. A rooster or a pig tattooed onto a sailor's foot could prevent him from drowning by showing him the way to shore.

Cats hold a special place in the magical thinking of seafarers. While a good mouser does help control rodents on a ship, some mariners ascribe magical powers to felines. Cats were believed to protect ships from storms, but they could also summon storms if the cat fell or was thrown overboard. Some beliefs led sailors to treat the ship's cat like a furry forecaster. If the cat sneezed, rain was on the way. If the cat was frisky, it would be a windy day. If the cat licked its fur against the grain, a hailstorm was coming. While these sailors' superstitions may sound absurd, there is method in them. Cats' sensitive inner ears allow them to detect changes in weather more acutely than other animals. They can sense the low atmospheric pressure that often comes before storms at sea, and this may cause them to act restless or nervous.

Later, in another show of superstition, Joey put out a fishing line as we were passing some warm eddies on our way toward the Gulf Stream. We had hit some sargassum, he said, a seaweed that brings with it the fish known variously as mahi-mahi, dolphinfish, or dorado. It didn't take long for him to hook something, and he let out a whoop as he began to play it. He tugged and released, tugged and released in that fisherman's dance of finesse and strength as he tried both to coax and exhaust the thing on the other end of the line. Then he jerked the line hard and began to pull it up, hand over gloved hand. The bright green-and-gold head of a small mahi-mahi peeked up over the rail, dots of bioluminescence glowing in the dark. Joey reached to pull it on board, and in that slippery moment the fish shook itself free and fell back into the water. "Shit," Joey said, and shook his head. "That ain't a good sign."

While we superstitiously waited to depart, though, Joey went over what he expected of us. Of the nine of us, only three—Joey, Damion, and Jen—had been hired as a professional crew. The rest of us were an ad hoc collection of hands with varying degrees of experience. It was important that we know how Joey ran his ship, since every captain does it a little differently. What is always true is that a ship thrives on routine, when all crew members know what they're supposed to do and when they're supposed to do it. Joey went over each task and its scheduled assignments: galley duty, head cleaning, deck swabbing . . . He went over the station bill, the listing of each crew member's duties in case of a fire or other emergency. He went over the watch, perhaps the most important job, which involved the entire crew. We had nine people, so there would be three watches of three people each. Watches ran around the clock and were either six or four hours, with the overnight watches being shorter. During your watch you were either at the helm, steering the ship; on the bow, watching for ships or other obstacles; or checking the bilge, which meant you were periodically checking to see if the ship was taking on water. A small amount of water in the bilge was normal, but any more than that needed to be reported, as it could indicate a problem.

As I listened to Joey, I thought back to my week on the *Clearwater*, and I wondered how that experience could possibly help me now. Every little thing I had done on the sloop had felt like an accomplishment, whether remembering the difference between port and starboard or hauling lines while singing sea shanties. There, we had always been within sight of the shore, the occasional Metro-North train chugging alongside us, fishermen and children waving as we sailed past them on our way to New York City. Every moment on the *Clearwater* had felt thrilling, because, I think, the balance was right. To feel a thrill, I had to be able to trust that a greater safety undergirded whatever danger I encountered. Here, the dial was pushed far beyond anything I could fathom. The things we would need to do as a team would take every bit of our energy and attention. But I did not know these people. I did not trust my own abilities. I could not reach the edge of the swimming pool and take a rest if I needed to. If the *Clearwater* was circus camp, with me balancing on a beam three feet off the ground, this was the real thing. I was walking the high wire with no net, and if I fell, I would take others with me.

Finally, just after midnight on Saturday, October 26, we set off from Muller's Boatyard in Mill Basin and began our trek to Bermuda. It would be a trip of eight days and 769 miles. I had $200 in cash, a credit card, and a one-way ticket back from Bermuda. As we motored out of Jamaica Bay, I looked back at the twinkling lights on the shore. The city, which to me seemed so grubby so much of the time, was transformed. The hard asphalt of the streets and the sharp elbows of the people had disappeared, replaced by the soft shadows of distance and night. The push-push energy was gone, too. Back there, the moment you stepped out your door, it didn't matter whether or not you had somewhere to be and were late to get there. It seemed that everyone else was, and you were simply swept up in their current.

Here, there was energy to be sure, but there was a stillness as well. The chaos and cacophony of the city were replaced by the singular order of the ship. It was a perfect, complete system unto itself. The curvature of the hull, its displacement of the water that suspended us, the torque and power of the engine as it rotated the shaft that turned the propeller that pushed us through the water—each of these functioned as if to provide a proof of physics, as if to say that, on this night at least, you could rely on the fragile balance of machine and nature and mechanics. This schooner was conceived, designed, and built for ocean waters. The sea existed for no other reason than to work with this wondrous vessel. Ship and water were a team, and we the people both controlled their relationship and relied on their getting along.

The first watch began shortly after our departure. As the least experienced, I was on with two of the most experienced, Joey and Damion. This was perfect, since I would have been on the graveyard shift back home and I was too nervous to sleep anyway. Joey was at the helm. Damion was at the bow. I was on the bilge. For a moment at the start of the watch, Joey let me take the helm. I could feel *Anne Kristine* coursing along with my hands on the wheel. It was nice. I felt myself breathe for what seemed like the first time since I had stepped on board. Joey took the wheel from me, and Damion headed for the bow. Since I needed to check the bilge only once every hour, I spent part of my time up front with Damion. We spoke little, content to look out at the darkness that stretched before us and to feel the gentle rise and fall of the bow as we cut a path through the calm waters of the Atlantic. I closed my eyes. I wanted to hear the sounds of the harbor before we reached open water—the city's hum in the distance, the gongs of the buoys, the clangs and honks of the bells and horns of tugs, pilot boats, and other working vessels as we passed. As we made distance those sounds faded, and we were left with the simpler sounds that enveloped us. The wind dominated, a white noise that blanketed everything around me. On top of that was the water, the rush beneath us accentuated by the lapping of waves as they hit the hull. And, finally, the reassuring sounds of *Anne Kristine* herself: the distant purr of the engine behind us; the gentle creaking of the wood of the hull, the deck, the masts; the flapping of the furled sails and the spiderweb of lines that crisscrossed the ship's expanse and disappeared up the masts into the darkness above.

The sounds and movement lulled me like a midnight ride on the New York subway, and the fight-or-flight adrenaline I had been living with the last several days drained away. I dozed and felt my body stop resisting the movement of the ship and start relaxing into its rhythm. I checked the bilge a couple more times and saw there was water down below, but not too much. This seemed to be the rule for wooden ships. I reported it to Joey, and we ran the bilge pump for a few minutes.

At 4:00 AM, our watch over, I said good night to Damion and Joey and staggered down the hatch. From the main saloon, I brushed past the foremast where it descended from the deck above and found my way along the companionway. I got to the port-side cabin where I had left my bag and, too tired to change, eased myself into the bunk fully clothed. Lying there, I tried to take in all that had happened. Two and a half days ago I had been sitting in a darkened auditorium listening to an adventurer talk about the unimaginable. I had tried to picture what would make a man leave the safety of the shore and trust a few meager strands of papyrus to hold back an ocean. And now here I was hoping that a few planks of wood would do the same for me. It occurred to me that it was not the boat that Norman was counting on to keep him alive, but the ten men around him. I wondered if I could count on these eight strangers and, perhaps more, if they could count on me. I resolved to make sure they could. I would bring the best of myself. I would listen to every order I was given, and if I did not understand it, I would ask questions until I did, however bad it made me look. I would use my actor's training to observe the more experienced sailors and copy the way they did things and carried themselves. And I would fight through my shyness to help build the connections that would make us a working group.

I felt I had made a good start with Damion and Joey. I liked them both, though I envied their ease around the ship, their confidence and swagger. I'd had this experience before when I had encountered working people in their own element, particularly those who worked with their hands in settings that seemed alien to me. As someone who had been raised with the notion that book learning was somehow superior to other kinds of knowledge, I greatly admired people who had earned their knowledge through experience and could do things that seemed almost magical to me. My carpenter friend who could transform a few pieces of wood into something beautiful and functional. The do-it-yourself auto mechanics in my neighborhood who spent hours tinkering under the hood every weekend. The vaqueros I had met in the Bolivian pampas when I had returned as an adult. Some had never been to school. They struggled to read and write, but they could braid leather into a lasso that would last a lifetime; they could track a lost calf and know precisely the copse of trees where it would most likely seek shelter; they could hear a Cessna well before you did and could tell you from the sound of the engine whose plane it was and which landing strip it was headed for. Joey and Damion were such men, and I wished I knew something, anything, as well as they knew a ship.

I dozed with these thoughts. We were tacking on the port side—my side—and as I turned toward the plank, I nestled in close. I could hear the water of the Atlantic Ocean rushing past us just a few feet from where I lay. I put my hand against the plank so I could feel the vibration. Then I closed my eyes and I . . . the ship . . . my fears . . . everything . . . disappeared.

I awoke several hours later to the unmistakable aroma of pancakes and bacon. My grandmother often surprised me with this special breakfast on my visits home. Was that where I was? I opened my eyes and saw the ship's ceiling plank a few inches from my nose. I felt the movement and heard the roar, and I snapped myself back to the present. Walking gingerly along the companionway, I found myself in the main saloon. I did not want to disturb anyone who might still be sleeping, but I need not have worried. Everyone was up, and the place was abuzz with activity. Barbara and Marty had breakfast duty and were in the galley stacking the pancakes and draining the bacon that had woken me up. Coffee was brewing.

Joey and Jen were studying a chart. Others were preparing the table for our meal. Both hatches were open, and fresh air and sunshine streamed in from above. I was struck by how comfortable and well-designed the space was. It made sense. The Bakers were planning to spend two years down there, after all. The galley was big enough for two people, and a large wooden table with benches could fit six easily, eight more snugly. A small bookshelf was stocked with well-worn paperbacks and a few hardcover books, mostly on nautical subjects. A simple sofa was adorned with throw pillows.

After breakfast, we began to hoist the sails—first the foresail, then the mainsail, the staysail, and finally the jibs, outer and flying, until every sail was unfurled. I was pleased my *Clearwater* experience was finally coming in handy, and when we were done, *Anne Kristine* was like a lotus that had just bloomed, delicate and strong and perfectly balanced. Peter turned to me and said, "Brother, you picked the right trip to come on. You sail a lot of crummy days for one day like this."

It turned out Marty was a gourmet chef, and good food kept coming. That first day, a lunchtime lasagna was a particular treat. Everyone gathered on deck, eating, taking in the sun, and warming to each other's company. I finally started to relax enough to get to know my fellow travelers.

Damion was just twenty years old, with sandy hair that fell to his shoulders, and looked every bit like the surfer that he was. He had grown up in Hawaii on a hippie farm "up *malco*," up the mountain, where they had grown their own food and hunted wild pigs. At seventeen he had talked his way onto *Edna*, and Joey had been grooming him ever since. It was clear they trusted and relied on each other implicitly.

Jen, the first mate and only other paid crew member, was a serious young woman who seemed more interested in getting to know her sextant than in getting to know any of us. She didn't seem too happy about the relative inexperience of the crew and our particular unfamiliarity with *Anne Kristine*, and she mostly kept to herself that first day. I hadn't ingratiated myself when I had lost my balance soon after the ship started moving and fell onto her lap like a ventriloquist's dummy. It was an awkward moment for both of us.

Peter Abelman and I had met at Norman's lecture, when he had looked my friends and me over skeptically. If he was still skeptical about my being along, he didn't let on. He was a knowledgeable and enthusiastic sailor, and he had the closest connection to the Bakers and the ship. It was clear he was the family's surrogate on the trip.

Barbara seemed like the kind of person you would want along on any trip. Her round, friendly face was quick to smile, and her affable manner put everyone at ease. She had sailed the Pacific with Joey and Damion and had sailed on *Anne Kristine* on some of the Novia Scotia charters. She had fed thirty people three meals a day on extended sails without breaking a sweat, which said a lot about her.

Marty, our chef, reminded me of other people I have known whose lives revolve around food, the making and the sharing of it. Both seemed important to him, and he carried his sturdy frame with lightness and grace. He was married with children and was thinking of moving to Hawaii and opening a restaurant there.

Laingdon was a last-minute addition like me, and perhaps because of this we immediately took to each other. He looked like he would have been at home in a Tolkien saga, with his scraggly beard and wire-framed spectacles. He had done most of his sailing up in Maine and had been the cook on the *Clearwater* the season before, which gave us something to talk about. Laingdon was friendly, but in a quiet, introspective way that appealed to me.

If we had been casting a pirate movie aboard *Anne Kristine*, John would have gotten at least a callback, as I could definitely imagine him letting loose with a couple of hardy "HARRRS!" before all was said and done. He reminded me a little of Ian Anderson, the wild-eyed flutist and front man for Jethro Tull, one of my favorite bands. His eyes weren't the same kind of wild, but they had a mischievous glint that made him look ready for whatever shenanigans might be in store. John had little sailing experience, but he could barely contain his excitement at being along.

And then there was Joey. A tad shorter than average height, barrel-chested, he had a broad nose and a head of thick, dark hair. Joey was born in the Bronx, but his family moved to South Carolina when he was seven. This made sense when I heard it—he had a Southerner's accent and charm, but just underneath there was grit and a native New Yorker's no-nonsense attitude. He seemed supremely at ease in his role as captain, with such confidence in his abilities and authority that he could afford to speak softly. I appreciated this about him, and I liked him for it.

There was a lull as the day wore on. In the early afternoon Peter had the helm. Laingdon was at the bow. Barbara was on bilge watch. Others dozed or daydreamed in the sun. Joey went below to check the latest weather faxes. I decided to inspect the deck, feeling a little like an airplane passenger who actually takes a few moments to locate the nearest exit and maybe even read the safety card located in the seat pocket in front of him. I walked slowly toward the bow, stopping often to keep my balance and holding the rail for support. I tried to take the measure of *Anne Kristine*. She had two masts. The mainmast about mid-deck, with the foremast, the shorter of the two, closer to the bow. Four hatches surrounded the foremast like sentries, and a mushroom vent sat near the port bow as if a visiting royal had left her crown. Two smaller vents rested toward the back of the ship, one to port of the helm and the other to starboard. Eight small prisms dotted the deck. Their purpose was to redirect sunlight to the ship's darker quarters, a safer alternative to the oil or kerosene lanterns used in bygone days. The prisms were complemented by a large skylight at center deck and a smaller one just in front of the helm. Two sliding hatches led below: one midships to the companionway, the other to the captain's cabin aft. The steering station was precisely three-quarters of the way back on the deck. Here the helmsman's bench and the wheel rested just behind the binnacle, a small wooden tower with a brass helmet on top that housed the ship's compass. It looked a bit like a Dalek, the noisy extraterrestrials from *Doctor Who*.

Finally, the davit jutted from the ship's stern, its two wooden arms holding up a small wooden lifeboat.

I stood back there, finally feeling my sea legs beneath me, and looked back at where we had come from. I missed my friends. I was having the adventure of a lifetime, but I wasn't sure I'd have the words to describe it to them. I wanted to have one moment that I could take with me, that I could report fully to everyone back home. I turned slowly, 360 degrees. Water in every direction, with not a spit of land in sight. I would try to remember this—the simple expanse as I looked into the distance with the horizon folding away, the sun on my face, the wind that seemed to overfill my lungs and made it hard to catch my breath.

While my original plan had been simply to survive the trip, it seemed the spell of *Anne Kristine*, the romance of being on the open sea, had begun to work on me. I didn't think of it at the time, but looking back now I am convinced that part of what I was feeling was the spirit of the Bakers, which imbued every corner and crevice of the ship. They—or those working closely with them—had bent every plank, buffed every surface, fitted every angle. Every bit of the ship was either original or authentic, re-created using the methods of shipwrights from earlier times. The evidence of this was all around, from the pinrails that held the belaying pins to the ratlines, the lengths of thin line tied between the shrouds to form a ladder up the masts. Everything on the ship had been restored, lovingly and painstakingly, by hand.

As I drank in the meticulous handiwork all around me, I was reminded of the experience of being in a museum alone, taking the time to become completely absorbed in a painting. In such moments I would stare so long at a Rembrandt, a Caravaggio, a Hopper, that I would feel myself looking not at the image but at the strokes of paint. I would imagine the hand that held the brush as it laid the paint on the canvas. Trying to understand the marriage of imagination, muscle, and medium that could create something of such beauty was almost too much to bear.

I began to think about those early sailors, the astronauts of their time, and I fantasized about what *Anne Kristine* might have been in her day. Schooners, smaller and speedier than their contemporary counterparts, were a revelation when they emerged in the late seventeenth or early eighteenth century. One tradition says the ship's name may have derived from the old Dutch word *schoon* meaning "beautiful," "fair," "fine." A more fanciful American origin story asserts that Captain Andrew Robinson, a Massachusetts shipbuilder, built the first of these vessels in Gloucester's Smith Cove. On the day the ship launched, it came down the ways and almost skipped like a stone as it hit the water. Robinson exclaimed, "Thar she schoons!" Or so the story goes.

The schooner's great innovation was the rigging of its sails. The square-rigged vessels that preceded the schooner needed to sail in front of the wind, with the wind, to catch it. They could turn into the wind, but only so much. Because its sails were rigged along the length of the deck, the schooner could catch the wind at a much closer angle and sail closer to the wind. In short, the ship's bow could be brought closer to the direction from which the wind was coming.

Its great speed, maneuverability, and economy—a schooner generally needed a smaller crew to operate—made it a favorite for seafarers of all stripes, whether fishermen, whalers, smugglers, or pirates. The latter appreciated the schooner's ability to negotiate craggy coastlines and dart into coves where larger ships could not follow.

My reveries got the better of me, and in my mind I began to create an adventurous past for *Anne Kristine*. The reality, of course, was far less swashbuckling. To be sure, she was the oldest continuously sailing vessel in the world, but that only took her back to the middle of the previous century. She was built on the Norwegian island of Halsnøy in 1868 as a *jakt* and christened *Stine Cathrine* for the owner's daughter. She was sold nine times and rebuilt twice, the second time after being struck and sunk by a German patrol boat during World War II. She was rechristened *Anne Kristine* in 1952. In 1973 she was sold to her first non-Norwegian owner, a Swede named Gjöran Grauers, who refurbished her in the Spanish Mediterranean. Grauers wanted to sail her around the world. He got as far as the Caribbean, where the Bakers found her in 1982.

As afternoon turned to evening on the twenty-sixth, we learned that the low-pressure system south of Bermuda was deepening. "What does this mean?" I asked. Joey said it was something we had to keep an eye on, but nothing to worry about. The system was five hundred miles away, tracking north and west, with winds around thirty-five miles per hour. We were still sailing full, all our sails unfurled, and *Anne Kristine* was handling beautifully. That said, something felt different, though I could not tell what it was. The atmosphere, both on the ship and beyond, had shifted. The air seemed heavier, more portentous. The wind blew harder and seemed to be shifting direction. Wavelets rose up higher than they had earlier, their crests breaking. Both the crests and the foam at the top of them looked like glass in the moonlight. Larger waves would occasionally appear. White horses, someone called them. On the ship, the mood had shifted as well. Though he was outwardly upbeat, Joey seemed preoccupied. He spoke quietly with Peter and Jen. Huddled at the table in the saloon, the three pored over the charts. From time to time, one of them would get up to monitor the radio.

I remained on deck, hunkered down near the helm, where Damion was steering. I hugged myself as the first funny feeling rose from my stomach. I felt dizzy, and saliva filled my mouth. "Damion," I said, "I don't feel so good."

"Dude, you're seasick."

What? How could that be? We had been sailing for the better part of a day, and while I had fallen all over myself (and several others) at first, I had finally gotten my sea legs. I had learned to relax my knees and waist, to go with the motion rather than resist it. I had reveled in the sun and the wind, and had even begun to fancy that I might someday become, not a Joey or a Damion perhaps, but a decent sailor in my own right. It seemed unjust, but there was no denying my condition. Marty called us down to dinner, but the thought of food, or even of going below deck, brought a new wave of nausea. I decided not to leave my spot near the helm, where the ship's movement was least pronounced. I pulled my knees in toward my chest and leaned back. Barbara brought me a blanket and some broth. I accepted the blanket, but the broth was more than I could handle. She left me a thermos of warm water that I sipped from time to time.

I have heard that seasickness has two stages: the first is when you fear you'll die; the second is when you're afraid you'll live. I went through both those stages that night, and probably added a couple more. Besides the physical symptoms—headache, dizziness, nausea—my mind reeled with doubts and regrets. How could I have imagined that it would be so easy? The day had gone too well, and now I would pay. *This* was reality: eight miserable days of feeling lousy and being useless.

As the wind played against my face, I breathed in as much of the fresh air as I could, using the technique someone had said would help with the nausea—a deep breath in through the nose, then a slow exhale through pursed lips. Over and over I breathed, trying to hold down the nausea that seemed to come up from somewhere beyond my gut. I was determined not to throw up; I had heard somewhere that this was the one thing you could *not* do on a ship, because it would start a chain reaction. Once one person lost it, everybody did. *OK*, I thought, *this is my new job. I can't hoist a sail or swab the deck, but I can do this. I will* not *lose it.* I could not make things better for everyone, but I wasn't going to make things worse.

———————

As the evening of Saturday the twenty-sixth came on, *Ernestina*, ahead of us and on a similar course, was still not experiencing storm conditions, but the reports were troubling.

From the ship log:

> **1930** *Motoring under fore and jumbo steering South. Swell building, wind still light, clear skies. Prepare storm trys'l for setting.*

The trysail is a small, tough triangular sail that flies behind the mast in place of the mainsail in heavy winds. It lets you preserve your regular sails while allowing you to maintain control of the vessel and helps keep your bow to the wind.

> **2100** *Set trys'l, main engine secured. Alter course to SxW, position 37° 36'Nx68° 18'W, to give more room to gale center. Wind NE'ly Force 2-3.*

"Force 2-3" refers to the Beaufort scale, a measure of wind speed based on the observation of the wind's effects. At 2 to 3 on the scale,

the breeze was still gentle, waves barely breaking, but the water's surface had taken on a glassy appearance that did not bode well. *Ernestina*
jibed slightly west, looking to put some distance between herself and
the deepening storm. The crew brought timbers up from below and
lashed them to the main boom, fitting a tripod beneath it to keep it
still. "The boom is a heavy thing," said Swanzey, "and if it starts moving around when you're moving around, that's horrendous."

Later, still on deck in the wee hours of Sunday morning, I looked up.
The sky was still clear and the moon, which had been full a few days
earlier, was waning gibbous. A cruise ship passed us on our port bow,
headed in the other direction.

6

SOUL OF THE HURRICANE

"A breath. A breeze. A whisper. Air moves to fill a void, and one thing leads to another."

—From my journal

WHEN JOEY TOLD US a depression south of Bermuda had deepened, it meant little to me. *Why should a far-off storm concern me*, I thought. Wasn't that what Joey and the other professionals were there for? Though I wanted to do my part as one of the crew, I didn't think I would be much use to them. I felt like a spectator. And while Joey's news did sound a little ominous, I had little doubt that those in charge would pull us through any difficulty. After all, I had been raised on television, the great spectator machine, and by the time I set foot on *Anne Kristine*, I had probably witnessed thousands of hours of creative unreality. None of this felt real.

For a brief time in my early teens, I had planned my entire schedule around programs that were designed to frighten me. Every evening (and often in the afternoon) I was mesmerized by *The Twilight Zone*, *Alfred Hitchcock Presents, Thriller* (hosted by Boris Karloff). I watched shows that promised to take me to *The Outer Limits* or *One Step Beyond*. I lived vicariously, and whatever mayhem flickered across the screen was always resolved by show's end, and I was always returned to the safety of my living room. Being on *Anne Kristine* felt a little like that, or like being on an amusement park ride: it had taken time to get my sea legs, and I imagined there might be some twists and dips along the way, but I never doubted that Joey and his assistants were in complete control of the ride.

Five hundred miles away, Grace was getting organized.

Hurricanes are among the most powerful, most destructive, most studied phenomena on earth, yet they remain largely a mystery. The devastating storms of the Caribbean and the Gulf of Mexico have always loomed large in the lives of the native peoples of those regions. For them, the great storms are part of the life cycle, deified, respected, and adapted to over millennia. For the Maya people of the Mexican Yucatán, Hurakán was the "heart of the heavens" and the god of wind, storm, and fire. He figured in their stories of both creation and destruction. In the lore of the Taino, the Caribbean natives, fraternal jealousy drove Jurakan, the god of destruction, to use a devastating wind to tear up the good things of the earth—the plants and animals—that his brother Yucaju had created.

The natives of this region have long known how to read the signs of an impending tropical storm, to feel the dropping air pressure and recognize the formation of cumulonimbus clouds that often bring the afternoon thunderstorms associated with the tropics—but that can also sometimes gang up into something far more sinister and destructive. But where does it all begin? To better understand the first flutters of many Atlantic hurricanes, we must go four thousand miles east to the jet streams of sub-Saharan Africa. There, small disturbances called easterly waves begin their trek across the ocean. "What triggers the formation of an easterly wave could be almost anything," according to Dr. Kerry Emanuel, a professor of atmospheric science at the Massachusetts Institute of Technology and a leading hurricane authority. "It could be a little girl playing in the sand, and that creates a little dust devil that perturbs the atmosphere downstream in such a way that you get one of these waves." These eddies of air, sometimes forming into systems of thunderstorms, travel west across the African continent, then encounter the warm tropical waters of the Atlantic. As the storms cross the ocean, they are fueled by the moisture and heat coming off the water. They grow. Soon, they begin to rotate around each other, the genesis of the familiar cyclonic vortex. From above, they look like tadpoles chasing each other in circles, closing in tighter as the storm gains force. As the heat comes off the ocean, the now fully formed heat engine converts that heat into mechanical wind energy. This is what powers the storm. Tighter and tighter it spins, taking shape, gaining speed and clarity, until an eye begins to form. The eye is an area of utter calm, but it is surrounded by the eyewall, a cylinder of activity that contains the storm's fiercest winds and heaviest rain. Get through this, and the cloudless, windless eye can fool you into thinking that the storm is over. Just the opposite is true. Soon, the other side of the eyewall follows, and you are slugged with the storm's worst winds again, this time from the other direction.

A mature hurricane is one of nature's most perfectly monstrous creations. In *Divine Wind*, his marriage of the science, history, and inspiration of hurricanes, Dr. Emanuel wrote, "The hurricane, once fully formed, is among the most coherent and persistent structures that inhabit the otherwise chaotic atmosphere of our planet. However terrible its effects, one cannot help but admire the intricate beauty of its architecture." This structure can be hundreds of miles wide and eleven miles deep, rising from the ocean's surface through the troposphere and into the lower stratosphere. It can move more than a million cubic miles of atmosphere per second and dump more than two trillion gallons of rain in a day.

Hurricanes create chaos. They devastate human populations, taking lives and destroying property. They decimate coastlines. They sink ships. But the phenomenon itself is the opposite of chaos. In fact, a hurricane is a supremely ordered system. It is an order that arises out of disequilibrium, of elements thrown out of balance that try to rebalance themselves by moving, converging, rearranging themselves into new and novel relationships. The primary ingredients in this apparent search for order are heat, water, and wind. Heat is the key; that is why hurricanes, also called tropical cyclones, form in that tropical band above and below the equator, where the water is warmest. As the easterly waves travel across the Atlantic, they encounter seawater that has been heated by the summer sun. This is the storm's fuel. As the water evaporates, it creates increasingly warm, moist, unstable air that rises and converges with the easterly waves and other winds that flow into this low-pressure area. As the air rises and condenses into clouds, heat is released, causing more ocean water to evaporate. Soon, a cycle is established. Water evaporates, rises into the storm, condenses when it hits cooler air, and releases heat, which causes more water to evaporate and rise into the storm. Like an enormous steam engine, the storm transforms the heat energy from the ocean into mechanical energy in the form of increasing winds. As the storm grows, the process accelerates. Because of the earth's rotation, the winds curve as they move inward, forming the familiar cyclonic spin—clockwise below the equator, counterclockwise above. The lower the air pressure at the center of the storm, the faster the winds that spin around it.

The storm, now a tropical depression with winds up to thirty-eight miles per hour, is off and running, and it will continue to grow—at an accelerating pace—as long as it has warm, moist air to feed it. As the storm grows, it pulls in more new fuel from the ocean surface and creates faster winds. It takes on a more defined shape, like an oceanic Catherine wheel. Once the spiraling storm's winds reach thirty-nine miles per hour, it is considered a tropical storm and is named by the National Hurricane Center. (That was the news we received about Grace on the afternoon of October 26, our first full day at sea.) If conditions hold, the storm continues to grow, and the winds continue to accelerate. A storm with maximum sustained winds above seventy-four miles per hour is officially a hurricane. Seen from space, it resembles a whirlpool of whiteness. It is at least fifty thousand feet high and 125 miles wide. A ring of its most violent thunderstorm clouds—the eyewall—spins tightly at its center, its centrifugal force opening a small column of calm all the way down to the sea: the eye of the storm. Dr. Emanuel often accompanies hurricane hunters, the aircrews that fly into tropical cyclones to gather weather data, but the experience still fills him with wonder. Of the storm's eye he has said, "Imagine a Roman coliseum twenty miles wide and ten miles high with a cascade of ice crystals falling along the coliseum's blinding white walls."

To fully appreciate the power and perfection of a hurricane, we might look back to a young French mechanical engineer of the nineteenth century. Nicolas Leonard Sadi Carnot was in the French army when, at age twenty-seven, he published his only book, *Reflections on the Motive Power of Fire*. In part, Carnot was motivated by a desire to imagine a more efficient engine than those that existed at the time. James Watt's steam engine, for example, wasted 80 percent of the steam it created. But Carnot's scope was considerably more ambitious. He wrote, "It is to heat we should attribute the great movements that appear to us on earth; to it are due the agitations of the atmosphere, the rising of clouds, the fall of rain." Carnot has been called the father of thermodynamics, and the engine he devised was groundbreaking in defining the thermodynamics of a heat engine: a Carnot engine imagines the perfectly efficient transfer of heat energy to mechanical energy. Being a "perfect" engine, it does not waste heat in friction or lose energy in changing the temperature of the other parts of the engine. Carnot realized that in the real world such an engine could not achieve 100 percent efficiency; there will always be an upper limit to its potential. His theorem stated that no engine operating between two heat reservoirs could be more efficient than a Carnot engine operating between those same reservoirs. In other words, Carnot's theorem specifies the limits on the maximum efficiency any heat engine can obtain.

Carnot's engine, like any heat engine, has three basic elements: 1) a high-temperature heat reservoir, 2) a low-temperature cold reservoir, and 3) the engine itself—for example, a cylinder filled with gas that expands and compresses, moving a piston as it does so. The Carnot cycle operates in four steps:

Step 1: The heat reservoir heats the gas in the cylinder just enough for it to expand at a constant temperature. The gas pushes the piston up. This is isothermal expansion, which means the temperature remains constant throughout the process.

Step 2: The heat is turned off, but the gas continues to expand and push the piston up. This is adiabatic expansion, "without the addition of heat." As the piston rises, the pressure on the gas is reduced and the gas cools.

Step 3: The cold reservoir is used to cool the gas. The piston falls, increasing the pressure on the gas. Again, the gas is kept at a constant temperature. This is isothermal compression, and the gas loses heat during this step.

Step 4: Finally, the cold source is removed, and the gas is compressed until it warms to the temperature it had at the start of the cycle, a process called adiabatic compression. The piston returns to its initial position, ready to start the cycle again.

In Carnot's ideal engine, all the engine's heat energy gets converted to mechanical energy; none is lost. By contrast, consider a real-world heat engine: an automobile's internal combustion engine. A car engine uses the heat of fuel ignition and the subsequent cooling to get work from the pistons of a car. As heat engines go, the auto engine is woefully inefficient. By some accounts, the average car converts only about 20 percent of the energy it produces through combustion into useful work, and even the newest cutting-edge models manage only twice that, about 40 percent.

A mature hurricane, on the other hand, turns out to be an almost perfect example of a Carnot heat engine. In this case, the ocean's tropical surface is the high-temperature heat reservoir; the atmosphere at the top of the storm, eleven miles up in the lower stratosphere, is the low-temperature cold reservoir; and the moist air, water droplets, and ice crystals of the storm replace Carnot's gas as the engine's working substance. To understand the hurricane engine's efficiency, let's follow a patch of moist ocean air as it travels through the cycle.

Step 1, isothermal expansion: The air begins near the sea surface, sixty miles or so from the storm center. It is drawn along the surface of the water toward the eyewall, the area of the storm's lowest air pressure. Like a roller-coaster car approaching the ride's first big climb, the air skims along near the sea surface, loading up on an enormous amount of energy from the ocean's vast heat reserves. Much of this energy transfer occurs from the evaporation of seawater into the inflowing air, greatly increasing the humidity of the air and adding energy to the air as latent heat. This is the most important source of heat driving the hurricane, and it occurs close to the eyewall, where the hurricane's winds are strongest.

Step 2, adiabatic expansion: Once the air reaches the eyewall, it is sucked up into this tight column of cumulonimbus clouds, the roller coaster spiraling upward in a corkscrew of pure violence. As the humid, energy-laden air shoots up this towering cylinder, its latent heat converts to sensible heat as the air climbs higher, the water vapor condenses, and droplets and ice crystals form. This stage exhibits an adiabatic expansion in which the air rises, but the total heat content remains approximately constant.

Step 3, isothermal compression: As the air flows upward, the pressure on it decreases rapidly, and by the time the air reaches the top of the storm in the stratosphere some eleven miles above the surface of the ocean, its temperature has fallen to about negative seventy degrees Celsius. The roller coaster has reached the apex of its ride, that breathless moment before the final drop. As it takes the relatively short ride from the stratosphere back to the troposphere, the air undergoes compression while at the same time losing heat to the surrounding space. The net result is that its temperature remains constant.

Step 4, adiabatic compression: Finally, the air sinks back through the troposphere. Along the way, the air loses heat by radiation to space, but this loss is offset by other factors, so the total heat content is preserved. The air arrives at its starting point, and the roller coaster is ready to begin the ride again.

Dr. Emanuel noted,

> The thermodynamic cycle of a mature hurricane is almost exactly like the idealized cycle envisioned by Carnot. . . . The hurricane Carnot engine, with its recycling of waste heat, is one of the most efficient natural generators of power on earth. The amount of power dissipated by a typical mature Atlantic hurricane . . . is on the order of 3 trillion Watts . . . enough to light 30 billion 100-Watt light bulbs.

Why do hurricanes occur? Humans have ascribed providential purpose to these storms from earliest days to explain the devastation they have wrought through the years. First, the gods were angry. Then, God was angry. But if we set aside supernatural reckonings, we are still left with questions. For one thing, the places where hurricanes happen exhibit—almost always—the most benign climate in the world. Many consider the isles of the Caribbean or the South Pacific heaven on earth because of their sunshine, gentle breezes, and cooling afternoon showers. And yet, as Melville famously put it, "Warmest climes but nurse the cruelest fangs . . . Skies the most effulgent but basket the deadliest thunders."

If we need a culprit, we might look to the sun. The sun transmits most of the energy that heats the earth, and a great deal of that energy is trapped in the ocean. The evaporation of ocean waters, along with convection—air currents that carry off much of the sun's surplus heat—help regulate the earth's temperature. Warm, moist air forms tall cumulonimbus clouds that carry the air upward, where the water vapor condenses into liquid water and ice, bringing the tropical storms that serve to cool things off. Most of the time the storm causes cool, dry air to come down to the earth's surface, and that is the end of it. The dry air is like a breath blowing out a candle. Sometimes, though, when the air is too warm and too moist, the air too saturated for the water to evaporate, the conditions are primed, and a hurricane can form.

But the truth is, the conditions necessary for a hurricane to occur exist most of the time in much of the tropics. Why, then, do they not occur constantly, or at least more often than they do? In this way, hurricanes do not behave like other meteorological phenomena. For example, when the conditions are right for a cumulus cloud, a cumulus cloud forms. Not so with hurricanes. Even if identical conditions exist in two instances, a hurricane might form in one and not the other. The reason why remains unclear. What is clear is that the occurrence of tropical cyclones—the collective name for what are called hurricanes, cyclones, or typhoons—is remarkably consistent. Globally, there are an average of ninety tropical cyclones a year, ten of which occur in the Atlantic or Caribbean. When we see that kind of consistency, it is a small step to discerning a pattern, and from there to recognizing a purpose. Scientists now believe these engines of destruction, these monsters of wind and water, play a vital role in maintaining the earth's delicate balance. They seem to do this in two ways. First, hurricanes help regulate the earth's climate by moving heat energy from the equator toward the poles, keeping the earth's temperature stable. Second, and less obviously, by cooling the tropical climate that spawns them, hurricanes may also be regulating *themselves*, siphoning off excess energy and making the next hurricane less likely than it would otherwise be. This self-regulating feature might be why there are ninety tropical cyclones every year and not nine hundred. (Climate change may be tipping this balance. At the time of this writing in 2020 there were 141 tropical cyclones worldwide, 104 of them named. The Atlantic experienced a record-breaking 30 named storms, of which 14 became hurricanes.)

Hurricanes do other useful things. While the rainfall that a hurricane brings can do a lot of damage, it can also be a boon to parched areas that need the water. In fact, parts of the southeastern United States rely on hurricane rains each year to replenish aquifers and recover from summerlong droughts. On the other side of the continent, moisture from decaying storms in the eastern Pacific is sometimes carried by east-blowing winds all the way to the deserts of California, Arizona, and New Mexico, regions that are often desperate for rain.

As a storm churns the waters through which it moves, it can break up bacteria and red tide in those waters. Red tide is the name for large concentrations of aquatic microorganisms that can kill fish and contaminate shellfish. It is prevalent along the Gulf Coast and the West Coast of the United States. The storm churn can break up populations of bacteria that lurk in the water and can bring an earlier end to the red tide. Hurricane winds can also oxygenate waters, helping return life to areas where the red tide once existed.

Barrier islands are usually the first line of defense against violent storms, standing like sentries outnumbered and outgunned by a vastly more powerful foe. After the storm, they often look it—battered and beaten, their sands diminished and their vegetation blown away. The truth is more complicated. While hurricanes do damage barrier islands sometimes, they can replenish them as well. As the storm approaches land, it picks up substantial amounts of sand, nutrients, and sediment from the ocean bottom and may deposit them on or near the barrier island. In fact, without tropical cyclones or artificial restoration, barrier islands would eventually shrink and sink into the ocean.

And the storm does not stop there. Its storm surge carries those same sediments ashore, providing footholds for new coastal vegetation. Its damaging winds flatten weak, diseased trees and allow tropical forests to rejuvenate. Those same winds disperse spores and seeds, and sometimes carry them thousands of miles from their source. Tropical hardwood hammocks—rich jungle groves originating in the Caribbean and Central and South American tropics—make a home with south Florida sawgrass glades and pine forests. West Indian mahoganies, gumbo-limbo, strangler fig, and others greatly diversify that region's plant life. While many of these seeds likely hitch a ride in bird gullets or ocean currents, hurricanes churning in from the Atlantic or Gulf of Mexico also provide transport.

Finally, hurricanes play a role in the function of the thermohaline circulation, the massive, slow-moving circulation of all the earth's ocean waters. Aptly called the "great ocean conveyor belt," the thermohaline circulation is the system by which all the waters of the earth's oceans get moved and mixed and replaced. It is a mysterious process, and oceanographers do not agree on what causes it. One thing we do know is that the process involves temperature ("thermo") and salinity ("haline"). The circulation continually replaces denser, saltier water deep in the ocean depths with less salty water from the surface and slowly replaces surface water elsewhere with water rising from deeper depths. A drop of water beginning in the North Atlantic will tour the globe, making its way south to the Antarctic Ocean, then east and north past eastern Africa to the Indian Ocean, where the conveyor bifurcates. From there the drop of water might go west, back in the direction from which it came, or continue east to the Pacific and around the other way. Along the way the drop will also travel up and down between deeper waters and shallower, depending on how salty it is at any given time. That means that the ocean water we dip our toes into, on a beach in Maryland or the Caribbean or out west in California, could have made its way there from the coast of Africa, Australia, or the Antarctic. It was a long, slow ride; some scientists believe one lap on the great ocean conveyor belt could take as long as a thousand years. Like so much about hurricanes, the exact role the storms play in thermohaline circulation remains a mystery, but it seems clear that the turbulence they bring to tropical waters is important. Without it, the warm layer of water that extends downward several hundred meters at tropical latitudes would settle into a thin sheet barely fifty meters deep, greatly reducing the overturning circulation.

———————

Hurricanes are among the most powerful natural occurrences on earth. They are among the most ordered processes. They are among the most beautiful wonders. Is it possible to see a picture of a hurricane taken from above and not be struck with its perfection, the delicate symmetry that spirals out from its eye, its solid core swooshing out to what seem like fluffy bunches of cotton candy? If only they were pink! It is impossible, I am told, to fly into the heart of the beast and not be swept up, quite literally, in its functioning, the peace of the eye surrounded by the utter, massive violence of the eyewall, energy being sucked from the ocean and shot upward, then flung out hundreds of miles, like the arc of Thor's hammer, leaving rain, lightning, and even tornadoes in its wake. Hurricanes are part of the system that keeps the earth in balance. Along with earthquakes, volcanoes, fires, and other natural events, they seem to arise in response to some disequilibrium.

They have been a part of earth's functioning for millions of years, much longer than humans have inhabited the planet.

We don't know how many lives were lost to tropical tempests in the Atlantic and Caribbean waters before the first Europeans arrived. The native inhabitants of the Caribbean and surrounding waters had been dealing with these storms for thousands of years before Columbus, but if they kept records of such events, those records have not survived. But the Europeans wrote things down. Columbus himself made three voyages without encountering a hurricane. By his fourth voyage, in 1502, he knew enough to recognize the signs of a storm approaching from the north. He secluded his ships in a harbor on the south side of Hispaniola and rode out the storm with little damage. Eighteen months later he returned to find that Santo Domingo, the city he had established, had been terribly damaged by that hurricane. Seven years later it would be almost destroyed by another.

Hurricanes have continued to strike that region, as they did for eons before. The difference is that, as the Europeans exploited this area for the riches it could yield, the stakes changed—the population grew, and the stage was set for the human suffering that these "natural disasters" would inflict. "Most people don't realize that the Caribbean was far and away the economic powerhouse of all the Americas for a long time," according to Dr. Emanuel. "And yet it's not that today, mostly because of hurricanes."

In the colonial Caribbean, the fortunes of the colonizers often rose and fell with the weather. One hurricane in 1565 wrecked the French fleet that was en route to attack the small Spanish garrison in St. Augustine, ending French efforts to take over Florida. Another in 1640 damaged a Dutch fleet before it could attack Havana, leaving Cuba under Spanish domain. In 1666 the British governor of Barbados lost most of his fleet in a hurricane near Lesser Antilles, leaving the French in control of Guadeloupe. A 1766 hurricane devastated Martinique, ruining the sugarcane business of a man named Joseph

Tascher. That caused him to send his daughter Rose to France, where she met and married Napoleon Bonaparte, who rechristened his new bride Josephine. Seven years later a hurricane hit St. Croix, where an impoverished Alexander Hamilton wrote eloquently about the experience. A collection was taken up to send the promising seventeen-year-old to the American colonies to study at King's College (now Columbia University).

And what are we to make of the numbers? In one month, October 1780, three brutal hurricanes ravaged the Caribbean and the Gulf of Mexico, killing over twenty-seven thousand people. These storms changed the economic and political history of the region and dealt a blow to the British efforts in the American Revolution. In the century that followed: 2,500 dead in Barbados; 1,000 dead in Puerto Rico and the Virgin Islands; 2,000 dead in Cuba; 1,800 dead in the Mississippi Delta; 2,500 dead in 1893 when Charleston, South Carolina, and many adjacent islands were destroyed. The twentieth century saw no respite. Like bookends of destruction, the Galveston hurricane (1900) and Hurricane Mitch (1998) together took over twenty thousand souls. In the current century, four hurricanes—Jeanne (2004), Katrina (2005), Stan (2005), and Maria (2017)—have claimed almost ten thousand lives among them.

And to be fair, these numbers are dwarfed by the toll exacted by tropical cyclones on the other side of the world and throughout history. When the Mongol emperor Kublai Khan mounted a sea attack on Japan in the thirteenth century, his vastly superior forces were defeated not by the Japanese samurai but by a massive typhoon. Twice. The Japanese decided that the typhoons must have been sent by their gods and so named them *kamikaze,* or "divine wind." In 1737 the Hooghly River Cyclone struck India from the Bay of Bengal, killing over three hundred thousand people. A century later, another cyclone and storm surge near the same river destroyed much of Calcutta (now Kolkata) and killed as many as seventy thousand. In 1923 Tokyo suffered the unimaginable—a typhoon swept through the city in the day, followed by an earthquake that night. Fires started by the earthquake were fanned by the typhoon's winds. In the end, 250,000 died. More recently, in 1970, a tropical cyclone took more than five hundred thousand lives in Bangladesh.

———————

At the end of August 2005, I listened to coverage of Hurricane Katrina on the radio. Standing alone in a kitchen in western Massachusetts, I could not turn it off as reports came in about what was happening in New Orleans. Correspondents reported from Baton Rouge, Houston, Mobile. There might have been someone in New Orleans itself, but it is hard to imagine that now. (How would they have gotten out?) It was like watching an accident I couldn't turn away from, if that accident took hours to unfold and got worse with every new report. As I listened, my mind flashed back to my own experience fourteen years earlier. I held on to the countertop and wished I were not alone, wished that someone would turn off the radio and take me out for a walk in the late summer sunshine. I knew I wasn't going anywhere on my own. I found myself asking questions of a New Orleanian I had invented in my mind: *Does the wind sound the same? Is the rain horizontal? Do you have a way out? Are you afraid?*

Hours later, I finally turned off the radio; in the days that followed, I learned the details that would make me feel moved and furious and ashamed in turn. Moved at the acts of courage and kindness as neighbors helped each other survive the storm that New Orleans had so long feared. Furious at the corruption, ineptitude, and stupidity at every level of government—from the local to the federal—that made the disaster so much worse than it might have been. Ashamed that the world had to see us this way. Katrina had blown away the thin white lie that the United States tells itself. The levees broke, and an entire city of mostly Black people was abandoned. One picture said it all: a Black man stands outside, water up to his waist. He holds a tiny baby in his arms. He stares at the camera not with anger or pleading but with resignation. It is as if he knows no one is coming. Not for him, not even for his baby.

At the height of the coverage, news outlets were estimating as many as ten thousand dead in New Orleans. The number of victims officially recognized by the state of Louisiana was 1,464; of these, over 500 names were never released. Many others were never accounted for.

Shortly after Katrina, I began working as a facilitator for Story-Corps, a national oral history project. We had a recording booth in Grand Central Station, and the public was invited to come in pairs to record interviews that would be preserved at the Library of Congress. As September wore on, I began to hear about the Katrina diaspora. Before the storm New Orleans had had a population of 484,600; more than half of the city's residents were displaced by the hurricane. Most of them evacuated before the storm; some made their way through the destruction and escaped the city in the days after. The majority went to Texas, California, and Florida; a smaller number ended up in New York. Two of them came to the StoryCorps booth on September 29, 2005, one month after Katrina. For me, they became the faces of New Orleans' loss and survival.

They were a Black mother and a daughter. The mother was in her late forties; her daughter was perhaps twenty-five years old. They both carried an expression I recognized. They looked dazed, displaced, as if they did not quite know where they were or how they had gotten there. They had been separated in the chaos of the storm. The mother had made it to Houston with most of the family; the daughter had hitched a ride to New York. They had just been reunited.

The daughter wanted to record her mother's experience of Katrina, much of which she had yet to hear. The mother was one of the people who had decided not to leave the city even after the mayor had issued mandatory evacuation orders. She and her husband had wanted to leave, but several members of the charismatic Catholic church to which they belonged were unable—or unwilling—to go. The couple decided to stay, and the group took refuge in the walled Catholic retreat center to which they belonged—formerly a convent for Discalced Carmelite nuns. The center's twenty-two-foot walls kept them safe from the wind and water that Katrina unleashed on the city. They heard sirens and cries. They saw fires in the distance. At first the mother's account was so quiet, so restrained, that my attention flagged. Then she began to talk about the decision to get out.

I noted as much in my facilitator's notes:

> A quiet account until she got to the part about leaving the city after the storm. Vivid images of cries in the night, a woman wearing heavy makeup and carrying a gun, people wandering through flooded streets, hungry and dazed. Good tape. They got in their car and left the convent to make their way to Baton Rouge. As they were leaving, and after they had seen so much devastation, they spotted a truck arriving with "fresh people," people come to help, and fresh food. On the side of the truck was a drawing of the fishes and the loaves.

In May 2006, just nine months after Katrina, I led a StoryCorps team that traveled to New Orleans. We set up our classic Airstream trailer in the French Quarter, a customized, soundproof recording booth nested in the back. The New Orleanians who visited the booth were of two minds: half wanted to tell their Katrina story, unburden themselves one more time and preserve their account in a recording. The other half wanted to talk about anything but Katrina. They welcomed the opportunity to sit in a quiet place and reminisce about better times. We had no agenda; we were there to listen. By then both mother and daughter had returned to their native city, and I contacted them. They came back to the booth to record a follow-up interview. They talked about all they had been through, about the kindness of strangers, and how good it was to be home. They looked better. The daughter was getting married, and they invited me to the wedding. I attended, aware that celebrations in New Orleans are special, and post-Katrina celebrations more special still. Death and music often seem to mingle in that city. It's almost as if folks figure, if they can't chase Death away, they might as well get him dancing.

Hurricanes kill more people worldwide than any other natural event. Cities, towns, and villages in vulnerable areas live in fear of their inevitable arrival. And while we use many words to describe these storms—*tragic, devastating, heartbreaking*—the phrase I see most often is a misnomer: *natural disaster*. There is no such thing as a natural disaster. Everything that happens in the natural world occurs for a reason. Some we understand; others remain a mystery. But they happen, for the most part, independently of our devices and desires. Hurricanes, as we have seen, perform several functions that help maintain the earth's equilibrium, and that is true of most of the phenomena we deem tragic when they intersect with human populations. Earthquakes occur when the planet's tectonic plates are out of kilter and move to restore a balance; volcanoes erupt to relieve the pressure beneath the earth's surface; fires often serve to purge a forest of old, dry growth and maintain its healthy biosphere. As the climate emergency progresses, and the prevalence and severity of storms, fires, and other phenomena trace back more directly to the effects of human activities, it becomes clearer that there is nothing natural about these disasters. They are unnatural disasters. They are human disasters.

A hurricane does not *care* about us. It does not keep track of the deaths it causes or the damage it inflicts. A hurricane that crosses an island with no human inhabitants is not a disaster; it's just weather. And yet, we give them names. We endow them with personalities, with intent. We romanticize them. The Europeans who first arrived in the Caribbean named Atlantic storms after the saint whose day in the Roman Catholic liturgical calendar corresponded with the day of the hurricane (for example, "Hurricane San Fabian"). When two hurricanes struck on the same date in different years, the hurricanes would be referred to by number as well as name ("Hurricane San Fabian the first" and "Hurricane San Fabian the second"). During World War II, military meteorologists working in the Pacific began to use women's names for storms, and in 1953 that naming method was adopted by the National Hurricane Center for use on storms originating in the Atlantic Ocean. In 1979 they started using men's names, alternating them with women's names. Storms are named in alphabetical order each season, a list of twenty-one names ready and waiting. (Names beginning with the letters Q, U, X, Y, and Z are not used.) When a hurricane is bad enough, its name is retired, out of deference to the storm's victims.

Strictly speaking, a storm earns a name when it becomes a tropical storm and retains the name if it becomes a hurricane. For example, in 1991 Tropical Storm Ana was followed by Hurricane Bob, then Hurricane Claudette, and so forth. Hurricane Grace was the eighth named storm of the season.

The 2005 Atlantic hurricane season, which included Hurricane Katrina, was the worst on record up to that point. There were so many storms, they ran out of names. When that happens, additional storms are given names from the Greek alphabet: Alpha, Beta, Gamma, and so forth. Hurricane Wilma, a Category 5 monster with peak sustained winds of 185 miles per hour, originated on October 15 and slammed into the Florida Keys shortly after. It was overlapped by two other storms, Tropical Storm Alpha and Hurricane Beta, that played out in the Caribbean toward the end of October. The twenty-seventh (and last) named storm of the season was Tropical Storm Zeta. It developed northwest of Cape Verde in the Caribbean on December 30 and did not dissipate until January 6, 2006, southeast of Bermuda.

Five hurricanes from the 2005 season caused enough damage and loss of life to have their names retired: Dennis, Katrina, Rita, Stan, and Wilma. That was the highest number ever retired from a single season, and the list included three of the top ten most intense Atlantic hurricanes on record (Wilma, number 1; Rita, number 4; and Katrina, number 7).

Disasters born of natural events are always the result of human actions and decisions. New Orleans' experience in Katrina is a perfect example. For starters, some have argued that the very existence of the city is an act of hubris—a city with an average altitude of six feet below sea level, in the wheelhouse of Atlantic hurricanes, is a disaster waiting to happen. In its history, New Orleans had survived fifteen hurricanes before Katrina, and the storm was the knockout punch many had expected would come eventually.

When StoryCorps arrived in May 2006, we did not know what to expect, and we spent much of our four-week stay trying to understand what had happened and what it meant to the city's future. When we weren't at the Airstream facilitating interviews, my team and I were calling or visiting community leaders, organizers, journalists, musicians, church pastors, Mardi Gras krewes, anyone who would talk with us about what had happened to their city.

When a natural event like a hurricane strikes, the cracks in human systems are revealed. In the case of Katrina, New Orleans ticked every box: inadequate infrastructure, poor preparation, inept responses. Racial, class, and other disparities sealed the deal. I had read about these issues in the past. Now, I witnessed their consequences firsthand.

One day we drove out to see the encampments that had sprung up outside the city, the temporary home of thousands of volunteers who had come from all over the country to try to help New Orleans dig out. Volunteers were helping residents clean up the slurry and debris that still blanketed thousands of houses all over the city. We accompanied a cleanup crew to a neighborhood of brick houses. Many were damaged, and the hurricane's detritus was everywhere—gutters, siding, fence posts, mailboxes. Everything that could be ripped away had been. As I watched the crew get to work, a thought struck me: this neighborhood was still in one piece. These were sturdy, middle-class houses that had stood up to the winds and the flooding. These were not the homes of the people we had seen on TV, the poor, mostly Black residents who had hunkered in the Superdome for days or been turned back by armed police when they tried to cross a bridge to safety. "Who's helping them dig out?" I asked. "What about their houses?" One of the volunteers told me, "There's nothing to dig out. Those houses are gone."

We drove to the Lower Ninth Ward, a poorer neighborhood with houses made mostly of wood, not brick. It is largely surrounded by water: the Mississippi River to the south, the Industrial Canal to the west, and a harbor to the north. The damage here was much worse. Storm surge had poured through breaches in the Industrial Canal flood protection system. Torrents of water had smashed some houses and torn others from their foundations. One of the volunteers insisted we go see "the house." This was a small, shotgun shack that had been lifted from its foundations and laid, intact, in the middle of the road. It was an absurd, disturbing sight. The house looked almost untouched, but it was, of course, an uninhabitable shell. For many, this became the symbol of New Orleans' Katrina debacle. Where was the family who had lived in this house? Had they made their way to the Superdome, the shelter of last resort? Had they managed to evacuate to Baton Rouge or Houston? Perhaps they had come back to the Lower Ninth and found a hole where their house had been, or found it here, in the middle of the road, and walked away.

A few days after Katrina, Kanye West, then a rising young hip-hop artist, famously said, "George Bush doesn't care about Black people." The comment, uttered on national television during a Katrina relief telethon, was lauded by some, condemned by others. But looking back at how Katrina played out, and looking at the list of the most vulnerable when a hurricane hits, it is hard to deny the statement's deeper truth. Black and Brown people. Poor people. Forgotten people. These are the people who are left in harm's way when a "natural" disaster strikes.

―――――――

A hurricane's story is first told by the National Hurricane Center. It appears, like dispatches from a correspondent, as a series of Tropical Cyclone Discussions, or TCDs. These short blasts provide a one-page assessment of what NHC forecasters know at the time and how they believe a storm will develop. These bulletins, issued every six hours, are intended for use by domestic and international meteorologists but are available to anyone. In conjunction with the TCDs, the Hurricane Center issues public Advisories and Intermediate Advisories every three hours. These contain information and are formatted to facilitate their use by maritime users. These are the advisories we received on *Anne Kristine.*

The first TCD for Grace:

> 1030 AM EST SUN OCT 27 1991
> VISIBLE SATELLITE IMAGES SHOW THAT THE SUBTROPICAL LOW HAS ACQUIRED ENOUGH CONVECTION NEAR THE CENTER TO WARRANT ITS CLASSIFICATION AS A TROPICAL STORM.

It went on to say that if the present trend continued,

> . . . SOME STRENGTHENING COULD OCCUR . . . AN AIR FORCE RESERVE UNIT PLANE WILL INVESTI-GATE THE STORM IN THE NEXT FEW HOURS.

In 1991 NHC reports were accompanied by an array of computer data, graphs, and pictures. Model input and model output data. Reconnaissance and satellite fix data. Files with provocative names like "Strike Probabilities" and "Minob Plots from Recon Flight Information." The TCD referred to the Global MRF Spectral Model, the Deep Layer BAM, and the NHC91, all state-of-the-art programs for predicting the formation and progression of tropical depressions, tropical storms, and, ultimately, hurricanes.

But none of these tools and systems could predict Grace in time to stop us leaving Brooklyn. None could foresee the storm that would descend from the North Atlantic. None could warn Norman or Joey that all their years of sailing experience or knowledge of the Atlantic storm season would let them down.

Norman told me later, "We timed *Anne Kristine*'s voyage south to avoid the November storms north of Bermuda and to avoid the hurricanes south of Bermuda. The common wisdom was that 'by October, it's over.' In fact, a hurricane supplication service is held in Lunenburg, Nova Scotia, at the end of October, a religious service thanking God for being spared from the hurricanes for another season."

Our first NHC Advisory:

> 1100 AM EST SUN OCT 27 1991
> ... TROPICAL STORM GRACE FORMS FROM LOW
> PRESSURE SYSTEM SOUTHWEST OF BERMUDA ...

7

DEEPER

"The hurricane is still tracking toward us on a NW'ly track but is expected to turn and pass off to the East."

—*Ernestina's* log

BULLETIN

NATIONAL WEATHER SERVICE MIAMI FL

11 AM EST SUN OCT 27 1991

. . . **TROPICAL STORM GRACE FORMS** FROM LOW PRESSURE SYSTEM SOUTHWEST OF BERMUDA . . .

SATELLITE PICTURES AND SURFACE OBSERVATIONS INDICATE THAT THE LOW PRESSURE SYSTEM WHICH HAS BEEN CAUSING GALE FORCE WINDS OVER THE SOUTHWEST ATLANTIC HAS NOW BECOME A TROP-ICAL STORM . . .

AT **11 AM EST** . . . 1600Z . . . THE CENTER OF GRACE WAS LOCATED NEAR LATITUDE 30.4 NORTH . . .

LONGITUDE 66.6 WEST OR **ABOUT 165 MILES SOUTHWEST OF BERMUDA**

GRACE IS MOVING TOWARD THE NORTH NEAR 10 MPH . . .

MAXIMUM SUSTAINED WINDS ARE **NEAR 50 MPH** . . . AND SOME STRENGTHENING IS POSSIBLE DURING THE NEXT 24 HOURS.

TROPICAL STORM FORCE WINDS EXTEND OUT-WARD UP TO 405 MILES FROM THE CENTER.

Sunday, 10/27/91
0700 *Sailing on a port tack with trys'l, fore and jumbo steering SW, wind ExN, force 5, cumulus clouds building, occasional sprinkle. —Ernestina's* log

On Sunday morning, October 27, in addition to the storm from the south, Captain Swanzey of *Ernestina* began tracking a nor'easter that was approaching from the north. That storm was also gaining strength. Although Grace was tracking north and west, the National Hurricane Center predicted it would turn east at some point. Swanzey remembered thinking, "We don't want to get into a place where there's stronger winds. So, let's go west, skirt the southern storm as it moves north." The only problem was that Grace was still moving west. If it did not change course in time, they would sail into the very heart of it.

———

While *Ernestina* was turning west, Joey decided to alter our course as well. Instead of a direct route to Bermuda, we charted a course slightly more southeast. In this way he figured we could skirt around the storm, which was southwest of Bermuda and was tracking north and west. According to reports the disturbance appeared to be nothing more than a depression, hardly something to be concerned about. This was our first mistake, though we did not know it at the time.

Joey called a meeting and told us the new plan. The day had dawned gray, and the winds and seas were stronger than they had been up to that point. But we had not lowered any sails yet, and as I looked around at people's faces, they didn't seem worried. In fact, I sensed a palpable charge go through us as we sat below deck. We were like a ball team getting a pep talk before the big game. I half expected Joey to tell us to put our hands in the center for one last cheer.

Anne Kristine shortly before our departure. PHOTO BY NORMAN BAKER

The truth is, sailors love storms. They may appreciate a day of clear sailing, but they will never sit around and tell sunny day stories. Scratch the surface, and you will get tales of gales, blows, worst days ever. Enduring a storm is how you earn your ship cred. You are a real sailor to the extent you have faced and overcome bad days on the water. So, it did not surprise me to see a smile on Joey's face as he spoke. Perhaps he had been concerned at the first reports of bad weather, but now he showed no doubt, no hesitation.

For one thing, Joey had confidence in *Anne Kristine*. He had not been on her for two years, but he knew she was a working ship. He had sailed her through squalls and heavy weather up and down the coast. He knew she could take a punch and keep going.

And Joey had confidence in himself. He had been to Bermuda several times. He had sailed across the Pacific and the Atlantic, taken people who had never been on a boat. He felt that if he had healthy, able-bodied people, "hands, literally hands, sets of hands, then I wasn't concerned at all," he said. "I knew Jen was a seasoned hand. I knew that Damion would go to the end with me." Damion looked excited. John, one of the least experienced among us, could barely contain himself. Now, he thought, we've got an adventure.

When I stumbled down the steps to the meeting, it was my first time below deck since feeling sick, and I was afraid I would succumb entirely in close quarters. But something happened as I listened to Joey. Maybe I was feeding off people's energy, or my own adrenaline was kicking in. Maybe the fresh air had done the trick. Suddenly, I didn't feel sick anymore. I was hungry, and I remembered that I hadn't eaten since the afternoon of the previous day. Marty heated up some water and made beef broth to keep everyone going since we weren't sitting down for breakfast. We would not sit down for a meal again.

Joey signaled to me and I followed him back on deck. He took the helm, and I sat nearby. I began to check the gasoline pump—the one they had bought before leaving—to make sure it was working properly. It had begun to rain steadily, and *Anne Kristine*'s bow rose and fell in rhythm as we sailed through white-capped waves. My sea-sickness was barely a memory as I put the thermos of beef broth to my lips. I sipped . . . and its flavor exploded in my mouth. It was as if I could *see* the taste of the broth. The beefiness. The brothiness. The very essence of it hit my taste buds and coursed straight to my brain, while the hot liquid cascaded down my esophagus to my stomach and from there to every other part of me, filling me with a feeling of warmth and well-being. I looked up and saw rain, individual droplets of rain careening horizontally through the air. I saw the wind. I saw *Anne Kristine* as if for the first time, saw how everything worked in unison—the hull and the masts and the spars and the lines. She was a good boat. She would take care of us. And I saw Joey. He smiled like a kid on a skateboard, the wind and water whipping off him as *Anne Kristine* sluiced through the growing waves. I took a long drink of broth and found . . . courage. Courage!

We were still Bermuda bound. *Anne Kristine* was sailing beautifully, and it seemed like the plan to sail around Grace would work.

By midday Sunday conditions had worsened—sustained winds of thirty-five miles per hour, wave height in double digits for the first time, probably ten to fifteen feet. The sea heaped upon itself, and the wind caught the white foam from the tops of waves as they broke, sending this spindrift swirling like phantoms around us.

We had been sailing full—all sails unfurled—since early Saturday. Now, trying to control the ship's speed and keep it stable in the heavier winds, we began to strike sails, beginning with the topsails. I watched in awe as Damion and Joey scrambled up the ratlines like a pair of Spidermen, fearless and sure-footed despite the wind and water.

Peter thought to himself that he would have waited to start bringing down any sails. He had sailed on *Anne Kristine* in those kinds of winds and worse without doing so. He was impressed by how beautifully she was moving through the water. "The boat was handling superbly," he remembered. "It was a lot of fun sailing, it really was." Joey seemed to be a more cautious sailor than Peter was, which was not a bad thing. But Peter missed having Norman there. When the two of them sailed together, it was a more collaborative give-and-take between two old friends. Norman was in charge, of course, but Peter felt comfortable asking questions and getting the master sailor's thinking behind his decisions. Peter learned a lot on those excursions. He was clear, though, that there was one person in charge here, and that was Joey. He had no problem with that. "I thought Joey was a good sailor, a real good sailor," he said, "a better sailor than I am."

Peter was on the radio and heard the noon forecast. The storm was bigger than we had originally thought and had been upgraded from a tropical depression to a tropical storm. It had been named Grace. This was a problem. Our juke to the southeast to end-run the storm was predicated on its remaining a relatively minor disturbance that would continue its path north and west. If it turned into a large storm, our present course would run us into its "danger" side. We would be sailing *into* the spin rather than away from it. Worse, a high-pressure system was developing in the North Atlantic and sending weather down from the north.

Peter came on deck. He wore a lightweight yellow slicker into the worsening rain and mist, but still had on his cutoff denim shorts and sneakers. Joey was up front tending to the sails with a group of us. Peter called him aside; this was best done in private. He updated Joey on the location and size of the storm, told him it had a name now, and said there was another storm coming the other way.

BULLETIN

NATIONAL WEATHER SERVICE MIAMI FL

2 PM EST SUN OCT 27 1991

... GRACE MOVING NORTHWARD ... BECOMING A LITTLE STRONGER ...

THE **CENTER OF GRACE** IS EXPECTED TO PASS TO THE **WEST OF BERMUDA** TONIGHT ...

AT 2 PM EST ... 1900Z ... THE CENTER OF GRACE WAS LOCATED NEAR LATITUDE 31.1 NORTH ... LONGITUDE 67.2 WEST OR **ABOUT 150 MILES** ... 240 KM ... **SOUTHWEST OF BERMUDA**

GRACE IS **MOVING TOWARD THE NORTH NEAR 10 MPH** ... 17 KM/HR ... AND THIS MOTION IS EXPECTED TO CONTINUE TONIGHT.

MAXIMUM SUSTAINED WINDS HAVE INCREASED TO NEAR 60 MPH ... 95 KM/HR ... AND SOME ADDITIONAL STRENGTHENING IS POSSIBLE DURING THE NEXT 24 HOURS.

Sunday, 10/27/91

1330 *The Gale is deepening and is not turning as predicted. We turn toward the west for more searoom on the gale without returning into the Gulf Stream where seas would be accentuated in a building NE'ly gale. —Ernestina's* log

As Sunday wore on, Swanzey had a decision to make: continue west or turn back to the east. Most Atlantic cyclones begin with a westerly trajectory. Of these, 75 percent turn back to the east. But hurricanes can be unpredictable beasts. They can change directions more than once or not at all. The forecasts kept predicting a turn east; it kept not happening. "But when we looked at the weather maps," recalled Swanzey, "at what's moving across the country in terms of low-pressure systems, high-pressure systems, the chances were something was going to push it back out to the northeast." Swanzey decided to go with the odds. At 1:30 PM, *Ernestina* took a hard right turn, trying to put some space between itself and the storm.

In turning west, *Ernestina* faced another dilemma. In addition to the storm approaching from the south, the nor'easter was sending gale-force winds from the North Atlantic. By turning west, Swanzey risked sailing back into the Gulf Stream, which they had passed through earlier. The clash of the Gulf Stream's flow *toward* the northeast with the winds descending *from* the northeast amplified waves and worsened turbulence at the nexus.

Although he was headed closer to land, Swanzey knew he didn't want to seek a port to ride out the storm. The safest place for *Ernestina* to be was out at sea, far from anything she might crash into. Swanzey wanted to sail west, away from Grace, toward the coast of North Carolina. Before reaching the Gulf Stream's western wall, *Ernestina* would turn south off the coast of Cape Hatteras and run parallel to the coastline from there. That would allow her to continue toward the Caribbean while staying clear of both storm systems.

———

On *Anne Kristine*, we were reducing our sails gradually, over the course of the afternoon. We struck the flying jib and outer jib, then reefed the main- and foresail. Reefing meant we shortened the larger sails, reducing their area by folding the bottom edge of the canvas in on itself and then securing it. This reduced the power of the ship and lowered her center of gravity, stabilizing her and making it easier to keep her on course in the growing seas. Reefing a sail is a precise procedure, but in most conditions it's no big deal for experienced sailors. They do it all the time. These were not normal conditions. Drenched from the rain and mist, and trying to stay vertical against the wind and the pitch, a group of us struggled to find the reefing points, grommets along the bottom of the sail. We took the lines that were permanently sewn onto the sail and threaded each through its corresponding reefing point. We folded the sail and tied it off. Well, the others did. I tried to help, but I was too busy holding on to one crew member, then another, as I tried not to be blown off the slippery deck.

Finally done with the mainsail, we made our way back aft, me wedged between Marty and Barbara and holding tight to the two of them. We turned to see Damion, who had gone forward to wrestle with some rigging that had come loose. "I was more than eager to do that kind of stuff," he told me. He wanted the adrenaline rush. The bow of the ship was rising and falling in rhythm like an aquatic metronome when it seemed to miss a beat. A moment later a wave cascaded across the bow and crashed onto the deck, catching Damion in its surge. For a moment he disappeared in a rush of green water that enveloped the deck. "Somehow I was able to hold on to the shrouds and have this thing blow by me," he laughed. "Whoever was on the stern deck, Joe, maybe a couple of you guys, were like, 'Oh my God.' That kind of stuff was happening every couple of minutes, man."

By dark we had struck the last of the sails. Despite the worsening conditions, it seemed we were still on the best course. At least, I was not aware of any talk of turning back or changing course. As Peter remembered it, "The boat was handling real well, and we were making good progress through the water. The seas were getting higher, but it was nothing really bad."

But things were about to get worse.

BULLETIN

HURRICANE GRACE ADVISORY NUMBER 2

NATIONAL WEATHER SERVICE MIAMI FL

5 PM EST SUN OCT 27 1991

. . . GRACE NOW A HURRICANE . . .

AT 5 PM EST . . . 2200Z . . . THE CENTER OF GRACE
WAS LOCATED NEAR LATITUDE 31.5 NORTH . . . LON-
GITUDE 67.8 WEST OR ABOUT 160 MILES . . . 260 KM
. . . WEST SOUTHWEST OF BERMUDA

**MAXIMUM SUSTAINED WINDS ARE NEAR 75 MPH
. . . 120 KM/HR**

Sunday, 10/27/91

1900 *The gale center has risen to wind speeds of a hurricane.*
—*Ernestina's* log

Another weather bulletin. Grace had been upgraded to a Category
1 hurricane with sustained winds of seventy-five miles per hour and
gusts up to one hundred. And what the storm lacked in wind speed,
it made up for in size. Grace was much, much larger than we had
thought. It would eventually become part of one of the largest storms
of the century—the southern end of what has been remembered in
story, film, and lore as the Perfect Storm.

Turning east to try to get around the storm had been a mistake.
We had underestimated the size and strength of the storm and had not
followed customary practice when confronted with a tropical cyclone

moving north from the Caribbean. We should have turned west. To the north, a high-pressure system that had developed in Canada was sending down a strong cold front that would stretch from Nova Scotia to North Carolina. We would soon be trapped between the two.

If the tropical depression had not developed into a tropical storm and then a hurricane, we might have been able to skirt around it to the east and reached Bermuda that way. If Grace had been smaller, we might have been able to avoid its worst effects. If the northern storm had come later or been less severe . . . If both storms had adhered to the common wisdom about Atlantic storms in October . . . If . . .

Every ship at sea is faced with a constant series of decisions that depend on conditions that are constantly changing. Nothing is guaranteed. You use your best judgment. But we had made the wrong choices, and nothing was breaking our way.

We made other mistakes that undermined the ship's ability to weather the storm. We failed to close the vents to the engine room and galley, and water came in that way. We didn't prime the pumps properly. Of the six pumps on board, only three were operating at all, and none to capacity. We had oil bags—the same ones that the Bakers' friends had given them in Tortola, the same ones that had helped the brigantine *Romance* survive a hurricane. You fill these cowhide bags with oil and puncture them. Then you tie them off with a line and toss them over the side of the ship. As the bags drag along beside the ship, they release a film of oil around its perimeter, and this keeps waves from forming because they can't build up enough tension. We used the wrong kind of oil.

Anne Kristine began to take on water. Afterward, people would disagree about why that happened. Some said most of the water was coming in from above, from waves that washed over open hatches and vents. Others said the ship was being "worked" so much—twisted and strained in the turbulent seas—that water was seeping in from below. The truth is, both are possible. She was an old wooden ship, and her taking on water in those conditions could be expected. But the pumps should have been able to keep up, and they did not. Several of us took turns working the on-deck hand pump until it stopped functioning. The small bilge pumps continued working, though they were not designed to pump high volumes of water. But the large centrifugal pumps worked at only a fraction of their capacity, and we never threw the valve that would have allowed the main engine to draw water from the bilge.

Joey had asked Barbara to take over below deck, to make sure people could have a hot drink or a bite to eat. Meals were out of the question. In the darkness I came below and sat down for the first time in hours. I wanted to eat something and get into my bunk. My next watch was at 7:00 AM, and I was exhausted. Laingdon, Marty, and John sat nearby, each one taking a break before going to spell the others. Finally still for a few minutes, I took the measure of the room, and for the first time I sensed fear, a palpable fear that had probably been rising in us for hours but that we had channeled into the go, go, go of the day's efforts. Now, in the pause, the wind and water churned like a spin cycle just beyond the hatch, and each of us sat silently, lost in our thoughts or simply too tired to speak.

Sunday night, we were still sailing to Bermuda. At least, that was what we told ourselves. I think we had to find some way to believe that things were still normal somehow, that we had run into a rough patch but would get through it. We would reach Bermuda as planned, if a little beat up.

But as the night wore on, I couldn't see how.

These were my last hours on deck, and they left me with my most vivid impressions: the color of each wave as it rose up—a deep blue turning green; the ship, which, had seemed so solid, suddenly picked up, weightless, frozen for a moment before crashing down; the moment at the top of a wave when the ship and I were both suspended, my breath in the middle of my chest; the sounds—the wind roaring around us and the timbers of the ship creaking below. The reason a wooden ship can withstand these conditions is because wood is so flexible. It will bend and give. But the wood screamed under the strain, and I wondered how much it had left to give.

And on we sailed, through the night.

Near dawn I was back on the gasoline pump. I looked up and saw Damion at the helm, Damion the surfer dude. As the ship tilted back and forth, he would bend one leg, then the other. And suddenly it occurred to me—he was surfing. He was riding the waves with a look of complete concentration and a crazy smile on his face.

BULLETIN
HURRICANE GRACE ADVISORY NUMBER 3
NATIONAL WEATHER SERVICE MIAMI FL
1030 PM EST SUN OCT 27 1991

... GRACE CONTINUING TOWARD THE NORTH-WEST ... NEAR 12 MPH ... 19 KM/HR ... AND THIS MOTION IS EXPECTED TO CONTINUE TONIGHT WITH **A GRADUAL TURN TOWARD THE NORTH AND THEN NORTHEAST** DURING THE NEXT 24 HOURS.

Conditions remained essentially the same through the night and the next several advisories—from 2:00 AM to 9:00 AM on Monday, October 28. Grace's maximum sustained winds held steady at seventy-five miles per hour, and the storm continued moving slowly toward the northwest. The forecasts kept predicting a turn to the east.

Monday, 10/28/91

0700 *We continue steering toward the west and Cape Hat-*
teras to avoid "Grace." The hurricane is still tracking toward
us on a NW'ly track but is expected to turn and pass off to
the East. —Ernestina's log

———————

On Monday at 8:00 AM Joey called another meeting. We sat in a circle
again, but this time it felt vastly different. I could feel Joey's eyes
searching ours as he spoke, looking to see what we had left, to see if
he could count on us to do what was needed. I struggled to meet his
gaze. Joey told us we were turning the ship around. We would sail
west to try to reach the Chesapeake Bay.

Joey's decision to turn the ship around lifted my spirits, and I felt
a sudden release. In my mind, in some strange calculus of survival,
that was all it should take. Everything would be OK now.

Overnight Laingdon had gotten horribly seasick, and we could
hear him moaning in another cabin as Joey spoke. I looked around
the circle, and I could feel the fear in the group rising as our empathy
drained away. Our shipmate was suffering, and I knew we should
care, but we just wanted him to stop. We did not want to feel what
he was feeling, could not *afford* to feel these things. We had to keep
working. With every moan we could sense the panic rising in us. He
had to stop, and we didn't really care what it took to shut him up.
Finally, somebody picked up a metal bowl for him to retch in and
went over to try to calm him down.

Joey took Damion, Peter, and Marty with him to work on deck;
the rest of us would stay below to support them. The hatch slammed
shut, and we were left in darkness.

8

DELIVERANCE

———

"You better start swimmin' or you'll sink like a stone."

—Bob Dylan

O N THE DAY he would come for us, Lt. Paul Lange paid little attention to the weather. The radio told him there was a storm well offshore, but it was a sunny day in Elizabeth City, North Carolina, and his shift didn't start until that afternoon. No need to borrow any trouble, he figured. Instead, he slept late so he would be well rested for work. He did some chores and played with his two young sons. Halloween was a few days off, and they were getting excited.

Lange knew from an early age that he wanted to fly. "Too many hours watching Superman on TV," he told me later. After four years waking up to his college roommate's Marine Corps recruiting poster, Lange signed up and went to flight school. But he struggled. He simply had no affinity for flying fixed-wing aircraft. Instead, he transferred to Whiting Field near Milton, Florida, the military's principal training facility for helicopter pilots. His first time in the cockpit, the instructor told him the three controls the pilot needed to master: the cyclic stick, collective lever, and antitorque pedals. Lange lifted off and held the helicopter in a perfect hover. The instructor gave him a target to fly to; Lange did so. The instructor told him to use the controls to turn left, turn right. Pitch up, down, left, right. The instructor asked him to return to Whiting and land the helicopter; Lange touched down perfectly. It was as if he was born to it.

"From that first moment, I never lost the bubble," he recalled, referring to the balance, like the bubble on a level. "My first best destiny," he said of flying helicopters. Lange flew twelve years for the US Marines, his last tour flying search and rescue (SAR) out of Cherry Point, North Carolina. He picked up jet pilots who ejected while on training flights. In 1988 he left the Marine Corps for the Coast Guard, where his father had retired as a Master Chief Engineman. By 1991 he had flown over five hundred SAR missions with the Marine Corps and Coast Guard. "Never lost anybody. Never hurt anybody," he said. "And you get a reputation for that. Crews want to stand duty with you."

———————

Joey came below to check the weather fax. In truth, Joey was everywhere—checking the engine, working the radio, making sure we were OK. It meant a lot to me that he had been through bad storms before. When did he realize we were in trouble? He never let on. As captain, he knew our best chance was to put us to work and keep us working. He told me later, "When it was really kicking up, you know, my thing was, 'Oh, is this bad? I've seen it three times worse.' I might go around the corner and say to myself, 'Goddamn, this is the one.'" But he was not going to let us see that.

Rather, he gave everyone a job. He knew Damion and Peter could steer, Marty was good with engines, Jen could navigate. The rest of us helped in whatever ways we could—operating hand pumps, spelling people, keeping up each other's spirits.

A low-pressure cell that had developed along the advancing nor'easter's cold front reached the surface of the water around the time that Grace reached its maximum strength. When it encountered Grace's warm air and moisture, the low stalled and strengthened. As it did, the storm produced titanic swells that would eventually batter coastlines from Maine to Puerto Rico. A government report would later describe this growing nor'easter as "an ocean storm of historic proportions."

For a time it would be called the Halloween Storm, and later the Perfect Storm. In meteorological terms, a "perfect" storm is one that could not be any worse.

Monday at noon Joey made a first call to the Coast Guard. At that point we were 368 miles east of the Coast Guard station at Elizabeth City. Joey told them that we were taking on water but were in no danger of sinking, and that we were attempting to reach the Chesapeake Bay. The Coast Guard dispatched a C-130 airplane to check on our position and our condition.

BULLETIN
HURRICANE GRACE INTERMEDIATE ADVISORY
NUMBER 5A
NATIONAL WEATHER SERVICE MIAMI FL
2 PM EST MON OCT 28 1991

... GRACE DRIFTING **NORTHEASTWARD** ...

AT 2 PM EST ... 1900Z ... THE CENTER OF GRACE WAS LOCATED NEAR LATITUDE 32.7 NORTH ... LONGITUDE 68.1 WEST OR ABOUT **195 MILES ... 310 KM ... WEST OF BERMUDA.**

GRACE IS NOW DRIFTING TOWARD THE NORTH-
EAST NEAR 5 MPH . . . 8 KM/HR . . .

MAXIMUM SUSTAINED WINDS REMAIN NEAR
75 MPH . . . 120 KM/HR . . .

———————

Monday, 10/28/91

1330 *The wind is rising rapidly now to NE'ly Force 8* [winds: 39–40 mph; waves: 18–25 ft] *as we strike the foresail and main trys'l and set a trys'l on the foremast with the jumbo set forward. We jibe to a port tack now to steer South parallel to the VA/NC coast 200 miles ENE Cape Hattaras* [sic]. *We cannot get pushed back into the Gulf Stream!*
—*Ernestina's* log

———————

Monday at 3:08 PM, Joey called the Coast Guard again. He told them our situation was worsening. Winds were seventy-five miles per hour with gusts to one hundred. Waves were thirty-five to fifty feet high. We were caught between the nor'easter and Grace, and we were taking on water. I could hear Joey's voice as he tried to give the Coast Guard a radar bearing on us. He counted, "1, 2, 3, 4, 5. 5, 4, 3, 2, 1." Over and over and over. His voice going out into the growing darkness.

As Grace reached its maximum strength, we had no choice but to run almost dead downwind of the storm. The full force of the hurricane pushed us from behind, down one fifty-foot wave and up the next. In those conditions the idea that we were surfing our hundred-year-old schooner in monster waves was no longer an analogy, it was a fact. And when you're surfing a big wave, your board—or your ship—has a tendency to turn off at the bottom of the wave. Turn off on your surfboard, and you've done a neat move; turn off on your ship, and the wave will roll you over. Joey, Peter, and Damion struggled to keep *Anne Kristine*'s nose pointed straight downhill. Joey described how:

> You get up on the wave and when you start to surf, you steer, you steer, and when it starts to veer off, you hit the throttle full bore and turn the boat dead downwind again, then back off the throttle. Then you crest up on the next hill, motor neutral, and start to surf. Surf, surf, surf, start to turn off—grrrrrraaahhh. Hit the throttle and do it again.

The guys fought hard as they tried to put some distance between us and the storm while bringing us closer to any help the Coast Guard might provide. Topside for the better part of sixteen hours, they came below rarely to sit for a moment and have a hot drink. It became a surreal experience, and not always a negative one. "The water was absolutely awesome," Peter said as he described waves that occasionally reached fifty feet. "It was a dark, angry green at the bottom and the tips were translucent and light blue. It was really quite beautiful."

The scene reminded Damion of paintings he had seen of sailors battling seas so violent they could exist only in someone's imagination, except that he was inside of it now. "At times it was like you were in the painting," he said, "part of that incredible, magnificent scene." He laughed. "That was like the hugest surfboard I had ever been on," he said. "We were screaming along, surfing some waves."

While Damion and Peter took turns at the wheel fighting to keep *Anne Kristine* on course, Marty crouched just to their left, nursing the Briggs & Stratton gasoline pump that Joey had bought just before our departure. The sturdy pump had been doing yeoman's work pumping water from the bilge, but waves from the worsening storm kept dousing it with salt water. Marty and others did everything they could to keep that pump alive, as it was the only pump on the ship that seemed to be making a difference. To help keep it running, someone would stand by the air intake on the carburetor with a can of starter fluid. Every time the motor started to bog down, they would revive it with a shot of starter fluid—all, of course, in hurricane-force winds.

The winds presented a particular obstacle when it came time to refuel the pump. We had a standard five-gallon plastic can of fuel. Peter said, "I remember getting the can and looking at Marty and saying, 'Marty, there is simply no way I can do this.' He looked at me and he had a funnel and I had this can." They could not get the can close enough to the opening of the pump's fuel tank without the gasoline being whisked away by the wind. Their solution was to bring the can below deck and funnel fuel into empty soda bottles. They could get a small bottle right up to the mouth of the fuel tank.

It was an elegant solution for the pump, but it was a disaster for those of us below deck. The gas fumes penetrated every corner of the space and hung there. After all we had been through, now we had to deal with new bouts of dizziness and nausea. At one point, Peter, clearly exhausted, came below deck for a short break. He placed the least wet cushions he could find along a bench and lay down. I said to him, "Peter, I feel like I have a gasoline nozzle in my mouth. Isn't there something we can do about this?" He squinted at me through a half-open eye and said, "Well, we could open a window."

Eventually, the gasoline pump failed entirely. The thin line of defense we had against Grace's onslaught was gone, and *Anne Kristine* continued to fill with water.

A sinking ship is like an hourglass in reverse: your time is marked not by falling sand but by rising water. By this time the water below deck was almost to our knees, and we were like crabs pummeled in the surf, falling all over each other as we tried to anticipate the next wave. Every step became several, like a complex dance that changed with the movement and sound around us—step, wait, step, step, step, wait, step, step, wait. The cozy space the Bakers had decorated with such care was laid waste. The books and mementoes of their travels that had lined the walls floated in the water beside throw pillows, flip-flops, and empty food containers. As the water rose, the ship's cramped quarters seemed to close around me even tighter, and I longed for the crazy exhilaration I had felt on the deck just a few hours before.

Joey waved me over, and together we went to the cabin where Laingdon lay. His seasickness had taken an alarming turn. As the seas got rougher and he'd gotten sicker, he had finally lost more than his physical strength—he'd lost his will. His worst moment came when he realized he was too weak to lift himself up from the floor. It was then he knew he might not be able to save himself, if it came to it. We found him curled in a fetal position, the metal bowl by his side. He looked bad, but in truth, he looked like I felt. The combination of fear and effort and exhaustion had caught up with me as well, and I wanted simply to lie down. I pictured myself in the bunk next to him, the two of us fading peacefully away. It was as if I were looking at us from a distance, and I couldn't muster an opinion about whether I should live or die; I just wanted to rest.

Joey leaned over and put his mouth by Laingdon's ear. "Hey, buddy," he said. "How you doin'?" Laingdon groaned in reply. Joey said, "Look, Laingdon, I need you. I need you to get up. I need you to get up and help."

I looked at Joey, who hadn't stopped moving in twenty-four hours; at Laingdon, whose eyes were finally open. I thought of my parents, who didn't know where I was, didn't know that they might never see me again. At that moment they were in Reyes, the village in Bolivia where my father had grown up. It would have been hot, the tropical summer not far off. It would have been another quiet, lazy day. Papi was probably getting up from his siesta; Mami might have been reading a book or sewing. She was certainly thinking of her children, whom she missed whenever she and Papi traveled. I thought of what it would do to them to lose a son. I pictured the moment they would be told, more than likely several days after the fact.

Joey and I helped Laingdon get up from his bunk. He was unsteady, but he managed to stay upright. We put him between us and went forward. Joey and John had taken the pump from the head and jury-rigged it so that we could lower the end into the bilge and pump out water by hand. Joey told Laingdon, "See that intake? Lie there and pump. And if you have to puke, you can just puke in the bilge."

I got down next to Laingdon, and we started. We were probably pumping next to nothing, but Joey had asked, and it was something to do, a place to put our attention. After a while, something told me it would be good to sing. And the songs I knew best were Bob Dylan songs. So I started to sing: a verse exhorting people to gather, to admit that the waters around them had grown.

I paused, and Laingdon and I looked at each other. We burst out laughing as he joined in. We sang out that soon

> You'll be drenched to the bone
> If your time to you is worth savin'

And then we screamed it, against the wind and the water and the creaking wood, as if by sheer volume we could hold back the storm for a moment.

> Then you better start swimmin' or you'll sink like a stone
> For the times they are a-changin'

And we sang, and we pumped. And we sang, and we pumped. "Mr. Tambourine Man"; "It Ain't Me, Babe"; "Blowin' in the Wind." All the old ones. And I could feel our spirits rising. And whenever

I felt us fading, I'd bring us back with another chorus. And on we went, into the night.

———————

Lange arrived at the Coast Guard Air Station at 4:00 PM and unfolded his six-foot, four-inch frame from his white Mazda pickup. He was a wiry man with prominent ears, an open expression, and an easy manner. As he walked toward the aviation safety office, he ran into Lt. Drew Pearson, the C-130 pilot who had checked on us earlier in the day. Pearson told him not to worry; the ship was well beyond helicopter range—even that of the new HH-60 Jayhawk the Coast Guard had recently commissioned. Besides, the ship's captain had requested assistance, not rescue. The ship was taking on water, but she was still sailing and was running west before the storm. "Looks like you might have a quiet night," Pearson said.

Lange went to his office to catch up on paperwork and catch a nap in case he was called out later.

BULLETIN
NATIONAL WEATHER SERVICE MIAMI FL
5 PM EST MON OCT 28 1991

... GRACE MOVING EASTWARD AND THREATEN-ING BERMUDA ... THE GOVERNMENT OF BERMUDA HAS ISSUED **A HURRICANE WARNING FOR BER-MUDA** EFFECTIVE AT 5 PM EST ... 2200 UTC.

REPORTS FROM AN AIR FORCE RESERVE UNIT AIR-CRAFT INDICATE THAT **GRACE IS NOW MOVING IN A GENERAL EASTWARD DIRECTION.** THIS EASTERLY COURSE MEANS THAT HURRICANE CONDITIONS WILL SPREAD NEAR BERMUDA DURING THE NEXT

24 HOURS. . . . PERIODS OF INCREASING TROPICAL
STORM FORCE WINDS SHOULD CONTINUE AT BER-
MUDA THROUGH THE NIGHT AS BANDS OF SHOWERS
AND SQUALLS CONTINUE TO PASS OVER THE ISLAND.

AT 5 PM EST . . . 2200Z . . . THE **CENTER OF GRACE**
WAS LOCATED NEAR LATITUDE 32.4 NORTH . . . LON-
GITUDE 67.5 WEST OR **ABOUT 160 MILES . . . 260 KM
. . . WEST OF BERMUDA.**

Monday, 10/28/91
1800 *We strike the main trys'l and sail under fore trys'l and
jumbo alone steering a SW'ly course and hear the response
by the US Coast Guard to a distress call from the Schooner
Anne Kristine 100 miles to windward of us.* —*Ernestina's* log

The *Ernestina* crew had lashed down everything that could be
lashed. They had sealed every opening they could. And still water was
coming in below. But even when the weather was at its most extreme,
Captain Swanzey never felt the ship was in danger. Wooden ships take
on water, that's the simple truth. "I've worked on plenty of wooden
boats, and they all took on water," he said. "It was not a surprise. But
you need backup systems and they all need to work. And so we were
diligent in that."

Ernestina had an engineer who knew how to keep the pumps
working. It had an experienced crew that knew the ship and its systems. And it had volunteers who continued to work, even through
the worst of the storm—thirty-five people in all, steering, keeping
watch, supporting each other so that none of the crewmates were ever
overwhelmed. If any ever were, there was always someone else to spot

them. As Swanzey recalled, "We just lashed everything down, held on, and hoped that we made the right decisions. Make sure everybody's safe. Everybody hang on. And the ship will take care of you. That's about it. That's what you do."

Monday at 6:39 PM, Joey signaled "Mayday," the international distress call. *Anne Kristine* was taking on more water than we could handle. Joey's plan was to put the rest of us into an eighteen-man life raft. He would stay on board to try to save the ship alone. After battling Hurricane Grace for twenty-four hours, besieged by the growing nor'easter, we were worn down and nearly worn out. We didn't know how much more we had left in us. And then something happened. Grace, whose steering was now dominated by the powerful flow of the nor'easter, made an abrupt hairpin turn and headed east, away from us. It was the break we needed. It gave us some distance from the heart of the storm, just enough to let us catch our breath. Joey soon rejected the plan to put the crew in a raft—at least for the moment. Launching a raft in those seas would be suicide. We would keep sailing and hope for the best.

Shortly after 7:30 PM our radio squawked again. The Coast Guard had dispatched another C-130, this one with three dewatering pumps. These were super pumps, any one of them powerful enough to empty the ship of the water she had taken on. Joey took the helm and told Peter to grab a boat hook and wait at the bow. He wanted Peter to be ready to snag the pump's line when it was within reach.

Joey said, "Be care—"

"Yeah, I know."

The ship's pitching bow was the most dangerous place to be, and even tethered Peter might not be safe.

At 9:50 PM Peter could see the lights of the C-130 in the distance.

Joey called out, "Pump coming down!"

What? Peter thought. *Where?*

They had dropped the pump to the wrong ship, a Danish trawler named *Tyborg*, two miles off our starboard bow. When he realized his mistake, the pilot asked the *Tyborg* to come to our aid. The captain of the trawler responded that he would, but we never saw them, and the Coast Guard never heard from them again.

The C-130 came back, flying just a hundred feet above the surface, trying to avoid *Anne Kristine*'s seventy-eight-foot mainmast as it pitched and rolled in the waves. They made fifteen passes, trying to get close enough to drop a pump within our reach. They dropped the second pump. Closer. Just behind us. But we could not go back. They buzzed past us a third time and dropped their last pump just ahead of us, its beacon light visible in the water and its line swirling in the waves as our bow approached. Peter plunged his ten-foot boat hook into the water below. He managed to snare the pump's parachute, but its weight and the force of the waves dragged him to the end of the bow. He gave one last, hard pull, but the pole was pulled from his hands and disappeared into the foam and churn below. He watched the blinking lights of the C-130 disappear as the plane rose to a safer altitude.

We were out of options. *Anne Kristine* was taking water over the starboard side, the gas pump had failed, and it seemed only a matter of time before the ship would founder or sink. The Coast Guard told Joey that a rescue helicopter was on its way. Our job was to keep running west to cut down the distance and to try to stay afloat. We hung a strobe light on the foremast to help them find us in the dark.

———

Lange was napping when the klaxon alarm went off. They were going. He had a half hour to get briefed, ready, and airborne. He ran to the on-duty officer (ODO) desk and got briefed on the case. The pump drop by the C-130 had failed. The ship's condition had deteriorated, and the captain wanted off. Lange huddled his team to figure out their fuel load, decide on equipment, get the latest weather, and do the flight planning. The ship was three hundred miles offshore, close to the H60's maximum range, so they called down to maintenance for a "full bag" of gas. When it came to getting fuel into an H60, no one could top it up like flight mechanic John Julian. To improve their fuel efficiency, Lange decided to remove the night sun, the 1.6-million-candlepower searchlight that hung from the copter's side; that would save on drag. Instead, they would rely on the H60's standard nose-cone searchlight and night-vision goggles.

Weather conditions were holding. Hurricane Grace was blowing at sixty-five knots (75 mph) with gusts up to eighty knots (100 mph). They would have steady crosswinds the whole way, ideal conditions for the H60, if you could call anything about a hurricane ideal.

About the H60: the Sikorsky HH-60J Jayhawk had replaced the old HH-3F Pelican just months before this mission. The H60 was the state of the art of what you could build to fly into a hurricane. Although smaller than the H3, it was much more powerful. The difference was like driving a souped-up Chevy truck into a storm instead of an old minivan. The H60 was also more technologically sophisticated than its predecessor, outfitted with the latest avionic devices and a flight control system that could hold course and altitude perfectly. Most important, the H60 had much greater range, speed, and reliability than the H3. In short, if this rescue mission had come up just a few months earlier and the H3 had been the only option, Lange would not be going anywhere.

Another thing Lange knew about a helicopter in a hurricane— especially one as solid as the H60—was that it loves the wind. An H60 in a hover in sixty-five-knot winds thinks it's flying at sixty-five knots. The wind does much of the work that the helicopter's rotors must do on their own when it's calm. Many things could go wrong on a case like this one, but Lange was confident it wouldn't be the copter.

Copilot Lieutenant Junior Grade Dave Morgan worked out the logistics. Morgan was an ex-army pilot who had been flying for the Coast Guard for four years. He was exceptionally good, unquestioned when it came to navigation, fuel monitoring, and systems management. Morgan was also steady and unshakable in the cockpit, the kind of copilot any pilot would want as his number two. The H60 was designed to fit six passengers in addition to the crew. Because there were nine to take off the ship, one helicopter would not be enough. Lange's copter would fly out and rescue as many as would fit. A second helicopter would launch an hour later and try to pick up the rest. Because there were no other flight teams on duty, the ODO went to random recall, the Coast Guard procedure for finding a crew for the second helicopter. "At that range and in those conditions," said Lange, "if anything at all went wrong, and we only got one or two people, there'd be seven people dead if we didn't have backup."

Of course, this is not what you think about when you are trying to get in the air. People who do dangerous work know how to compartmentalize. They become task-oriented: first do this, then do that. Then do the next thing. Lange and crew boarded the helicopter. The captain, cocaptain, and flight mech were joined in Hangar 49 by rescue swimmer Duane Jones, a strapping young man from Texas.

Lange finished his preflight checklist and fired up the APU, the auxiliary power unit that was used to start the H60's twin engines. The copter roared to life, and Lange began to taxi to the launch pad. He flipped the switch for the searchlight and . . . nothing. The light, which had checked out minutes before, was out. He set the parking brake and maintenance replaced the lamp quickly; everyone knew moments lost now could cost them at the other end. While maintenance fixed the light, Julian topped up the tank to replace the fuel they had burned during the repair. They would need every drop.

Finally ready, Lange lifted off again, only to find another problem. The needle on the radar altimeter gauge was not working. This was a crucial malfunction, because it left him with only a digital readout, which might be difficult to discern in turbulent conditions. With their departure already delayed, Lange faced a decision: Should he risk the viability of the mission by landing again and spending still more time on the ground, or should he take his chances with the equipment they had? Lange decided to forgo the needle, believing digital would be sufficient. This would become a challenge later when the high seas made the digital readout just a blur of rapidly changing numbers. Fortunately, the photoluminescence from algae in the water gave sufficient light even on a stormy night to judge the hover height. He pulled back on the collective lever, tilted the H60's nose down slightly, and flew off into the night.

Lange and company left without knowing who the crew of the second helicopter would be or when they would launch, but trusting that they would follow close behind. They would later learn that a crew headed by Rob Austin left Elizabeth City on schedule, one hour after Lange's departure, but they ran into their own much worse difficulties soon after launch. They lost their tactical data processor, a piece of equipment so essential that two are installed in every helicopter in case one goes out. The TDP controlled the radio, navigation, radar—everything but the searchlight and intercom. Austin lost both TDPs. He was flying into a hurricane at midnight, and he was blind, deaf, and dumb.

As Lange left the shore, he flew over the Currituck Beach Lighthouse, which he knew was on a direct line between Elizabeth City and the scene of operations. He had memorized the latitude and longitude coordinates of each lighthouse along the coast as a way of checking the accuracy of his old LORAN navigation system. The advent of GPS had made navigation almost infallible, but his old habit still reassured him. He passed Currituck, glanced at the GPS position. All good. Just then, he heard Morgan's voice in his helmet earcups.

"Paul, we're not going to make it."

"What do you mean?"

"We're gonna have to turn around ten minutes before we get on scene."

The winds were worse than they had figured, and their fuel would not be enough to complete the mission. Lange didn't need to check the numbers. "If Dave said it, that's the way it was." They would need a lily pad, something to land on and refuel, but not just any Coast Guard cutter with a little helicopter pad on the back. In those conditions, they needed something larger, at least a landing platform helicopter (LPH) or landing helicopter assault (LHA)—Marine Corps helicopter carriers with at least ten landing pads. Morgan radioed the base, hoping for help.

Pete Stein answered. Stein wasn't supposed to be working. He had come in to catch up on some paperwork and found the new ODO—who was working his first shift alone—overwhelmed. Stein had pitched in to help and never left. Now, he listened to Morgan's assessment and began making calls, searching for surface assets somewhere in the helicopter's vicinity. Lange continued flying on course in the unlikely hope that the weather would change or a refueling ship could be found. Stein went through all the normal channels to find someone within range of the H60 who could take them in and top up their fuel. He found no one.

That's when he picked up the Secure Telephone Unit. The STU-III (this was the third generation) was an encrypted phone developed by the National Security Agency in the 1980s. It was the closest thing to a hotline the Coast Guard had. He called the naval base in Norfolk, Virginia. The navy captain on the other end was "less than helpful," as Stein remembered it. "And I guess I had some kahunas for a lieutenant, because I said to this captain, 'Do you mean to tell me that because of a storm, the United States Navy has left the east coast of the United States unprotected?'" There was a pause, and the voice on the other end said, "Stand by."

The call was transferred, and moments later Stein was speaking to the captain of the USS *America*, an aircraft carrier that was riding out the storm a hundred miles off the coast of Virginia. Stein briefed the captain, and the captain answered that if the helicopter pilot was crazy enough to be out in this weather, his ship would go to flight quarters and fuel him. Stein relayed the carrier's coordinates to Morgan, and Lange adjusted his course, heading for the *America*.

The *America* lay 100 miles away from the H60, 250 miles away from *Anne Kristine*. As they traveled, Lange talked with Lt. Cmdr. John Schoen, the pilot of the C-130 that had tried—and failed—to drop pumps to *Anne Kristine*. Schoen updated him on the ship's coordinates and conditions on scene. One of the challenges for Lange was that, for all its technological wizardry, the H60 had a terrible radio, so bad that the helicopter could communicate with most other receivers—the air station or the *America*, for instance—only when the two were close enough to be in each other's line of sight and could use the ultra-high frequency (UHF) radio. The C-130 was flying above the storm, so Lange always had a line of sight on it. With the others, as soon as the curvature of the earth got in the way, they would have to switch to the high frequency radio, and the H60's HF radio failed them again and again. Over the course of the 7.6-hour mission, Lange spent hours at a time with no radio contact with anyone.

While Schoen was on scene, he provided communications support for Lange and his team, relaying messages between the helicopter and the ODO in Elizabeth City. When Schoen got low on fuel and headed back to the base, Lange was left with no radio contact and no way to communicate with the air base or the aircraft carrier. Morgan put out a call on a hailing frequency, searching for contact, essentially calling out into the storm's howling winds, "Is there anybody out there?" An Air Force hurricane hunter answered. Hurricane hunters are research planes (usually C-130s) that fly X-patterns through hurricanes at different altitudes. Among other things, they measure the storm's strength and direction of travel. This one was nearby and began relaying messages back to shore and to the *America*.

Lange got a fix on the carrier. And then he saw it. He had seen many aircraft carriers before, but he had never seen a boat pitching like that. "It's taking spray over the bow," he said. "It's taking seas along the catwalks." Big as it was—over a thousand feet long and weighing 62,000 tons—it was getting beaten up. Its vast steel deck was empty, wiped clean, with not a plane or person in sight. Then, his headset crackled, and he heard a voice. It was Morgan.

"We can't land on that."

Morgan was from the army and had never landed a helicopter on any kind of amphibious vessel. In the Coast Guard, you either landed on land or on water—in fact, the H3 was an amphibious craft, designed to land on water. They practiced that rescue maneuver all the time. But you didn't land your copter on a big slab of steel that was rocking like a wobble board in, well, a hurricane. Lange, the ex-marine, was an old hand at this kind of landing. He shot back, "Don't worry. I've got it." He knew the secret for landing on a boat is not to land on the boat. You must let the boat land you. Lange buzzed down and held the H60 in a position just above the deck of the rocking ship. He knew the deck would eventually rise and touch his wheels. When he felt it, he bottomed the collective to bring as much weight on the deck as possible to keep the copter from sliding.

Once down, Lange and company waited . . . and waited. Where was everyone? After a while, the navy fuelers (called grapes because of their purple overalls) came out. They were harnessed and secured to the deck by belaying lines but were still blown around as they ran the fuel line out and filled the H60's tanks. Even the captain of the ship came out on the bridge to wish the rescue crew well. "We'll be here when you get back," he told them. Within minutes Lange, Morgan, Julian, and Jones were back in the air and on their way to get us.

BULLETIN
HURRICANE GRACE ADVISORY NUMBER 7
NATIONAL WEATHER SERVICE MIAMI FL
1030 PM EST MON OCT 28 1991

... GRACE THREATENING BERMUDA ...

A **HURRICANE WARNING** REMAINS IN EFFECT FOR BERMUDA.

AT 1030 PM EST ... 0330Z ... THE **CENTER OF GRACE** WAS LOCATED NEAR LATITUDE 31.7 NORTH ... LONGITUDE 66.1 WEST ... OR ABOUT **90 MILES ... 145 KM ... WEST SOUTHWEST OF BERMUDA.**

GRACE IS MOVING TOWARD THE EAST SOUTHEAST NEAR 14 MPH ... 22 KM/HR ... AND THIS MOTION IS EXPECTED TO CONTINUE WITH A **GRADUAL TURN TO THE EAST TUESDAY AND NORTHEAST TUESDAY NIGHT.**

Shortly before midnight, Joey came below deck and said, "It's time to go." And I immediately went back to my bunk and started packing. Joey, exhausted after more than thirty hours awake, shook his head. "No, Nelson," he said with a laugh. "Your life. Just your life." *So, what do I take with my life?* I took my cash. I took my credit card. I looked at my keys. Would those few ounces make a difference? I left the keys.

After reaching *Anne Kristine*'s vicinity, Lange received a radio call from the base telling him about the system failure on the second helicopter. It wouldn't be coming, and Lange was to save as many of the crew as he could. He moved into position a hundred feet above the water and seventy yards off the ship's port side, fighting to hold onto his control stick in the storm's buffeting winds. He needed to hold the hover as still as possible. It was important for the flight mech and swimmer to sense that the hover was under control; it meant a good chance of getting everyone back on board. In weather like this the pilot will always ask if the swimmer feels safe deploying. It is a formality; the swimmer always says yes.

Behind Lange, Jones and Julian prepared to go to work. Jones had pulled on his swim mask, snorkel, and fins. Julian had assembled the 2-by-3½-foot metal rescue basket. From here forward, Julian would be Lange's second set of eyes. The pilot turned off every other radio channel, leaving Morgan to monitor communications. He would listen only to his hoist operator, who would guide his movements for the rest of the mission.

Joey laid it out for us. There could be no rescue from the deck—no way for the helicopter to get close enough. We would jump into the water, one at a time. The helicopter would pick up that person and come back for the next one. It would do this nine times.

We opened the hatch, and I followed Laingdon, Barbara, and Jen onto the deck. It was the first time I had been on deck in fifteen hours. And it looked like some bizarre site-specific performance piece. Above us it was pitch black, except where the helicopter hovered off our port side, its spotlight bathing the ship in a deathly white light. Below us the sea had its own eerie glow where the churning waters had released algal phosphorescence. I looked at the faces of my friends. And I know this was not possible, but it *felt* still. I had my harness on. I had my life vest on. Each of us had a light and a whistle.

The order would be Laingdon, Barbara, Jen. I would be fourth.

Laingdon had rallied from the worst of his seasickness, even help-ing topside in our final hours. But he was left weak, and Joey wanted him off the boat first for his own sake. Laingdon unclipped from the jack line, climbed up on the port-side rail, and held on to the nearest line. The H60 flashed its spotlight, the signal that they were ready. Laingdon stood there, trembling, not jumping. The rest of us watched, not breathing, some of us holding on to the closest person as we tried to keep our feet. Joey stood below Laingdon, his face turned up to him, his hands on the rail. Laingdon looked down and said something to Joey that we couldn't hear. But we heard Joey.

"Laingdon, you can do this. Every second you stay, we have less chance of getting off the boat."

Laingdon answered something. Joey said, "I need you to jump."

"Jump!"

And he was gone.

The H60 peeled off. We could see its spotlight in the distance as its crew searched for our friend.

Inside the helicopter, Lange and his team initiated the standard procedure that had been perfected over thousands of rescues, using an economy of standardized words to avoid confusion. Lange sighted Laingdon in the water and went into a hover thirty feet above him. Julian talked him into position. The idea was to get Jones in the water as close to Laingdon as possible.

"Forward, forward. Left. Hold." Then,

"Swimmer's ready. Swimmer's in the door. Swimmer's going out the door."

Below the helicopter, Jones dangled on the hoist line as Julian low-ered him toward the foaming seas. As soon as he felt the water close around his legs, he released his harness and plunged beneath the waves. He came up and tried to get his bearings, looking to get hands on the survivor as quickly as possible. He grabbed Laingdon like a puppy, lifted him up by the scruff of the neck and in one powerful motion deposited him into the basket. Jones flashed the thumbs-up, and Julian hoisted the basket. The swimmer remained below until Julian could lower the basket again to bring him up. The first rescue had taken ten minutes.

"That's not good enough," Lange thought. Their fuel window was an hour on scene, and there were eight people left to pick up. He had to make things go faster. The easiest way to do that—though not the safest—would be to hover closer to the water. He would reduce his hoist altitude from thirty feet to fifteen. The waves were high but far enough apart that Lange could hop over them as if he were flying low over terrain.

Morgan radioed Joey to let him know Laingdon was in the copter. "Get the next one ready."

On the ship we were queued at the rail like movie-ticket buyers. Barbara was next. She tried not to think about the funky little life jacket she had on—the kind that just fit over her neck rather than her entire torso—or about the sharks she was sure were lurking beneath the waves. When Joey called her up to the rail, she joked about doing this in tandem. Joey said, "You ready, Barb?"

"Sure, Joe."

She jumped without giving herself time to think about it.

Again, the H60 circled back. They were on her quickly, within thirty seconds. The basket came down and she tried to climb into it face on. Jones appeared as if from nowhere and swung her around, lowering her as if placing a baby in a cradle. Barbara looked back at her rescuer in awe as the spray blinded her and she ascended, leaving him below. Better this time.

Julian hoisted Jones up. The swimmer shuffled toward the door and gave the thumbs-up to indicate he was ready to go again. Julian said, "Wait a minute." Something wasn't right. Jones was on all fours, vomiting. A wave had thrown him deep beneath the surface and he had fought his way back up. In Coast Guard parlance, he was "mamucked up." Could he continue? Jones insisted that he could, but it was obvious to Julian that the diver was in no shape to go back in the water. He told Lange, "He can't go again."

Lange radioed Joey and told him we would have to get in the basket ourselves. Joey told him we would. What choice did we have?

I watched as each of those who went before me jumped and was quickly enveloped in the darkness and the waves, bobbing as each swell lifted them up like a cork. It seemed uncertain that the Coast Guard helicopter would find them, and I was surprised at how quickly they shrank to a small, vague point excruciatingly far away, then disappeared entirely as *Anne Kristine* kept barreling forward. In that moment something hit me: we were becoming separated. As scary as the last thirty hours had been, the nine of us had gotten that far together, working together, fearing together, always finding consolation in the fact that, however hopeful or dire things seemed—and they seemed everything at one point or another—we had been each other's appendages, thoughts, chances. Suddenly, we were forced to trust in someone and something outside ourselves, and each of us had to do it alone.

After Jen jumped, Marty approached Joey. Both he and Peter had been overwhelmed with helplessness and despair since the helicopter arrived. "It was the first time it hit me that we were losing the ship," Peter said later. "When I realized that I was going to have to leave her, I felt physically ill." Now with Laingdon and the two women safely off, they both wanted to stay and save *Anne Kristine*. Marty said, "We can still do this, Joe."

Hearing this, I felt like raising my hand. Had they forgotten that *I* was still on board? Surely, they had made this proposal a little sooner than intended.

The three stood in a small group and talked while I tried to wish the helicopter back. Joey listened, but he had made up his mind. One of the worst things he could imagine was not bringing Norman back his ship. But the worst thing he could imagine was losing anyone in the attempt.

Finally, it was my turn.

Joey motioned to me, and I came forward. I unhooked my harness. I stepped up on the rail. I looked up at the light. And I jumped. I jumped, tensing myself against the chill of the water, but there was no chill. It was the Gulf Stream! In that moment, a feeling—utterly, wonderfully surprising—of calm spread through my body. After thirty hours of fighting to stay alive, I didn't want to fight anymore. I needed to let go and let someone else fight for me. Or not. I would live or I would die, but I would finally do one or the other. It was the not knowing that I couldn't take anymore. I don't remember if I was afraid. I bobbed up. The rush of movement, the warmth of the water. And again, the stillness of time. I came up to the surface and felt no urgency, no desperation. I decided I could stay afloat for as long as necessary. I turned on my light and watched the spotlight in the distance, approaching.

Minutes later, I poured myself into the basket and focused on the open helicopter door, my deliverance, above.

We were on a roll. Lange and company had adjusted to the conditions on scene, and our crew, as we had all day, did what was asked of us with a minimum of fuss. Jump off our ship in the middle of a hurricane in the middle of the night? Sure. Stay afloat in ridiculous seas until a helicopter can find us in the dark? Not a problem. Lift ourselves into a two-by-three metal basket that's getting blown and thrown around by wind and waves? As you like.

Which is not to say there were no more problems. To hit us with the basket in those winds, Lange had to bring the H60 right down to the water's surface, timing each wave so that he could hop over it as it rolled by. Sometimes, he was so low that waves would lap at the helicopter's wheels. "And nobody wants the tires to get wet," said Lange, "because the engine intakes are just a little behind them." On each descent, Lange listened for Julian's voice on his headphones. A frantic "Up, up, up!" and he would yank hard on the collective, the black lever on his right that would lift the copter to a safe altitude. Each time, the helicopter's gears shrieked and groaned as he overtorqued the engine. But the H60 never let him down.

Once inside, we lay on the floor of the cabin and huddled together as close as we could, for warmth and contact. I was cold, wet, and more exhausted than I could have imagined. I buried my face into someone's back and wept, knowing that no one would notice in the darkness and din around us. I was struck by a strange lottery feeling as we watched the door to see who the basket would offer up. Although the alternative was unthinkable, there was an unmistakable sense of gambling, winning each time the basket came up full. Who would be next? It became a little game as I watched, knowing that anything less than a perfect score meant tragedy—and I felt a growing buoyance and near celebration in my chest as our rescued ranks grew.

Each of us came up in turn—Marty, John, Damion, Peter. Finally, Joey appeared at the opening of the helicopter. He was in the basket, and he had a belaying pin he had taken from the ship. Those of us who could, looked out of the helicopter, and we saw *Anne Kristine*. With no one at the helm to keep her sailing through the storm, she turned, as if offering herself to the waves, went over, and down.

The helicopter, overloaded but managing well, turned and headed up, away from the surface of the water, the nine of us a soggy pile on the cabin floor. I must have slept, because I woke up when I felt the helicopter touching down, not on land but on the deck of a large ship. Lange had flown back to the USS *America*. Nearby was another Coast Guard helicopter, which turned out to be the lost second copter. Their TDP was still out, but they had managed to get close enough to the *America* to be picked up by the ship's radar. They had then flown triangles with one-minute legs, the signal for a lost craft with no radio. The *America* vectored Lange over to the backup H60, and he had led them in. The weather had improved. The *America*'s deck was much more welcoming this time.

Two hours later we touched down at the US Coast Guard Air Station in Elizabeth City, North Carolina. The winds had diminished, and the rain had stopped. Ringed by the crews of the two rescue helicopters, our motley group—dressed in paper robes and pajamas—entered Hangar 49. There, a hundred people were waiting, Coast Guard people who realized this was no ordinary mission.

Lange strode in and raised his right arm in triumph.

"Got 'em all!"

The place erupted.

Someone led us into an office and, on Tuesday, October 29 at 3:50 AM, we made the hardest call, perhaps, that any of us had ever had to make.

Norman answered, and Mary Ann was on the other line. Joey said to them, "We're ashore."

Norman said, "Really? How is *Anne Kristine*?"

"We're on land."

"Where's *Anne Kristine*?"

"We're on land."

"Where is *Anne Kristine*?"

No answer.

We were crying. They were crying. And there was nothing anyone could do.

After the call, the Coast Guard put us in a van, in our pajamas, drove us to a nearby Holiday Inn, and left us there. I was in a room by myself. It was 5:00 AM. Exhausted and wired, I paced around the motel room, unable to sit down, much less sleep. I wanted desperately to talk to someone and tried to think of who to call at that hour. Of course! I called the law firm, my friends on the graveyard would be near the end of their shift. I talked to Nora. She said, "I told you not to go."

I finally slept a little, then walked around in a fog that would last for weeks. We asked at the front desk where we could get some clothes, and they told us about a discount jeans place down the road. We went en masse, looking like escapees from the asylum. I bought a pair of cheap jeans, a flannel shirt, sneakers.

I don't remember the rest. Somehow, I got to the airport. Somehow, I got on a plane. Somehow, I got home. My grandmother opened the door again and said, "What are you doing here?" I said, "I'm sorry." And I collapsed.

The morning after our rescue *Ernestina* continued to sail parallel to the coast on a south-southeasterly course 180 miles southeast of Cape Hatteras. Winds were blowing at fifty miles per hour and seas were still high, but there were signs of moderation. By that night they learned that a low-pressure system crossing Quebec had combined with Hurricane Grace and the nor'easter, and the storm was regaining strength. Swanzey and his battered crew had had enough. With the seas to the north growing more complicated and better weather to the south, they decided to forgo Bermuda and instead plotted a course for Puerto Rico. The ship had indeed taken care of them. They were intact and, except for an engine that had been flooded with salt water, all systems were functioning.

On Saturday, November 2, they were able to restart the main engine and run at three-quarter speed steering for Puerto Rico. Bermuda lay 250 miles behind them, and their destination was 600 miles away.

Once we were gone Grace continued its acceleration eastward and reached its peak intensity later on the twenty-ninth, topping out as a

Category 2 storm with sustained winds over one hundred miles per hour. It met the nor'easter, and like a punch-drunk boxer picked up wind and waves and staggered west again. Finally, on October 30, the growing nor'easter absorbed Grace entirely. The clash of the cold air from the north and the warmth and humidity from the remnants of Hurricane Grace strengthened the nor'easter and spawned yet another hurricane, this one unnamed. Together, these massive, unpredictable storms wrought havoc on the Atlantic from Bermuda up to Nova Scotia.

———————

Ernestina had sailed away from all that.

> Tuesday, 11/5/91
> **2100** *We lay at anchor in anchorage "D" off Club Nautico, San Juan, Puerto Rico!—Ernestina's* log

9

AFTER

"On days when I sing with duende no one can touch me."
—Juan Peña Fernández, "El Lebrijano,"
flamenco singer, on duende, the inspiration
that comes when one confronts death

I KEEP GOING BACK TO THE PICTURE. Somehow a photographer got us all to stand for it on the balcony of the Holiday Inn, one of our last moments together before we spun off in a half dozen directions. We are still wearing the robes and pajamas given to us by the crew of the USS *America*. What makes it so remarkable? For starters, there are nine of us. That is the first imponderable. If anything had gone differently . . . If Grace had not turned sharply east, giving us a respite . . . If Paul Lange and his crew had not been so skilled . . . If we had not kept our heads and stuck by each other . . . If any one of a thousand tiny details had been different, there might have been seven of us in the picture, or three—or a shot of the North Carolina coast, gray clouds, storm surge, and a caption about a ship lost at sea with a crew of nine. Missing, presumed dead.

Then there is the photograph itself. It is so poignant, it looks staged. Joey is at the center. He and Damion, who is just behind him, do not—cannot—look at the camera. They were the last two to abandon *Anne Kristine*, and it's almost as if they have left the deck of the ship but have not quite found their way back to shore. Their bodies are with us, but their spirits are in transit. Barbara and John are to Joey's left and right, quiet smiles on their faces. Barbara looks serene, almost beatific. When Joey told her it was time to jump, she had joked about doing it in tandem, then jumped without hem or hesitation. Here she looks as if she would do it again in a heartbeat. The others—Jen, Marty, Peter, Laingdon—appear as four heads in the background, like kids craning to get themselves into the family holiday picture. I am just behind Joey and John, my hair wild, my glasses too large, my eyes hooded, half-closed.

The last crew of *Anne Kristine*, hours after our rescue. From left to right: John, Nelson, Joey, Marty, Peter, Damion, Laingdon, Jen, and Barbara. UNKNOWN

Each of us looks a little different, but if you showed the photo to some passersby, who don't know us, don't know our story, and asked them to describe the people in this photo, they would say we all look like we have been through something. Something big.

When did we get separated? It had been almost unbearable to leave each other the first time, to jump into the abyss and trust that we would not be alone for long. Now we fell away without knowledge or recognition, with barely a muttered goodbye. What was there to say? See you later? Nice knowing you? Nothing could convey the enormity of both gratitude and embarrassment we felt in the aftermath of the rescue—gratitude to each of the other eight for keeping us alive, embarrassment at having been that vulnerable with each other. It was like two strangers who fall in love on an elevator stuck between floors. Suddenly they feel the gears engaging, the movement. The doors open, and they exit with averted eyes.

We were like ghosts, barely aware of our own existence, trying to make our way home.

Later I learned that Peter and Laingdon had flown back to New York, though not together. The others had rented a car and driven back to western Massachusetts. The rescue had made the news, and people knew them wherever they stopped. "We ate for free all the way back to Berkshire County," John told me.

I must have made it to Norfolk Airport, where I used my credit card to buy a ticket to DC, though I don't remember this. It never occurred to me to go back to my apartment in Brooklyn. In my mental state, surely descending into the initial numbing stages of shock and grief, I could only point myself toward my one real home: my family. My parents were still in Bolivia, but my grandmother and my sister were back in Maryland. I would go there.

Nothing could throw Nazira. My maternal grandmother had grown up on her father's ranch in the pampas of Beni, Bolivia. At a time when women were relegated to tending the house, Nazira tended the cattle alongside her father and his men. She loved to remind me that she could outride and outshoot most of them, and she had once accompanied her father on a cattle drive to the Brazilian border—a trip of over a month—on which they had lost most of the cattle and had barely survived themselves. After she married my grandfather Roberto, a Bolivian military man, she had embraced him and that life with the same fierce devotion she'd had for the family of her birth. Through a series of postings to mosquito-plagued backwaters, and even into exile in Argentina to escape a coup attempt, Nazira looked after her little family—which by then included her daughter, Mami, and son, José—like a mama *tigre*. She would take care of me.

Once I was home, I did the only thing I could. I slept. For two days I slept, getting up only to eat occasionally. Abuela seemed happy to have me, though a bit mystified even after I had explained everything. My grandmother was a supremely practical person, and she was often exasperated by her grandson, who too often lived with his head *en las nubes*.

Eventually, I got up and began talking with friends back in New York. How was I, they asked. When was I coming home? I *was* home, I thought. I didn't see any point in heading back to Brooklyn. What would I do there? I was in no state for anything. Soon I learned that the Bakers had decided to host a gathering of *Anne Kristine*'s extended family at their home in western Massachusetts. Part memorial, part celebration, it was a way for Norman and Mary Ann to find some solace amid their grief and confusion. They wanted the ship's final crew to be there.

The news tipped me over from numb exhaustion to utter hopelessness. I had left my driver's license aboard *Anne Kristine*. I could not rent a car to drive to Massachusetts, and the nearest airport to the Bakers' home was Bradley International, seventy-five miles away. All was lost, and I wandered the house for a day making sure my grandmother and sister understood how unhappy I was. Finally, Fatima took me aside. Gently, she told me to stop moping around.

Did I want to go, she asked.

"Yes," I answered. "Yes."

How important was this?

"I have to be there," I said, "but . . ."

She held up her hand. No buts. And with a seventeen-year-old's piercing clarity she solved everything. I would make a reservation. I would fly to Bradley. Once there, I would hire a car service to drive me the seventy-five miles to the Bakers, whatever the cost. I stared at my sister. As soon as she said it, it seemed obvious. I felt like a man who has been living in darkness, is taken by the hand, and is led to a window to gaze upon the sun.

A plane trip and a hundred-dollar cab ride later, I pulled up in front of the Bakers' home near Pittsfield and immediately wondered what I had been thinking. I was completely out of place. Over a hundred people had shown up to reminisce, grieve, and console the Bakers. It was as if a beloved child had been lost, and the family's closest friends had descended on their home to comfort and protect them. I wandered into these proceedings like the friend of a friend.

As a result, I spent the afternoon wandering from room to room and between indoors and out, explaining who I was and recounting the story repeatedly once the person realized I was one of the nine. The rest of the crew had already been there a day or two, and the time I would have wanted—private time to connect with them and Norman and Mary Ann—had happened the night before. Now things were wrapping up. Someone took a picture of the nine of us as people headed for their cars. I realized I had not planned beyond getting to the Bakers' home. I had no return ticket home. Someone had an extra space in a car headed for New York, and I took it.

While at the Bakers', I became aware of something—an impulse, a tension—running through the gathering. People were talking. In groups of two and three, never loudly or openly, people had begun to wonder, speculate, express doubts about how and why *Anne Kristine* had been lost. What did I know? I was happy just to be alive. For me, the narrative was simple: We left Brooklyn. We ran into an unexpected storm of unprecedented proportions. We fought to stay alive. We were rescued thanks to the skill of a courageous Coast Guard crew and by the grace of God. End of story.

But the story was just beginning. A day or so after the rescue Norman sat down with Peter, his close friend, to get his account of the trip. Peter had been on the charts and the radio much of the time, and he reconstructed our route as best he could. He told Norman what decisions had been made and when. He acknowledged that he did not agree with the captain's every decision, but in the end only one voice mattered. Peter said, "I may have lost the whole crew, but I would never have left the ship. Joey was thinking of the crew. I can't argue that point. We're here."

Norman also talked to Joey. He asked him about the decision to head east instead of west when we first became aware of the storm, about the operation of the pumps, about the implementation of the oil bags. Over the course of several hours, Norman asked his captain to take him through every moment of the journey, every thought, notion, or question that crossed his mind. More than anything, Norman wanted to know why Joey had not called him for help. Norman felt sure he could have saved *Anne Kristine* had he been there, and that he could have talked Joey through every crisis we confronted. Of all the questions around the loss of *Anne Kristine*, this one haunted Norman the most. In a letter to Jen, the first mate, he wrote, "Once the ship was lost, we were called immediately, even though it was 4:30 in the morning. How different it would have been had I been called twelve hours earlier. Even six hours earlier."

Soon after, Norman traveled to Elizabeth City to meet with Coast Guard officials and get their version of events. Perhaps he still held out hope that *Anne Kristine* could be found and salvaged. If so, he was disappointed. The ship was under thousands of feet of water, its exact location unknown. Even with the exact coordinates of the rescue, deep sea currents could have taken the schooner anywhere.

Norman and his family were devastated. It would be easy to compare the loss of *Anne Kristine* to the death of a child or a sibling, and just as easy to dismiss this as hyperbole. But it is the only comparison that helps me understand what they went through. It was a loss that followed Norman the rest of his life. In 2016 I invited him to attend a presentation about my experience on *Anne Kristine*. Afterward, when asked a specific question about a particular technical point, he spoke for twenty minutes about *every* aspect of the loss of the ship. These were facts he did not strain to remember after twenty-six years. He lived with them every day.

As painful as was the loss of their ship, the Bakers never forgot the miracle of our rescue. In a letter to friends they wrote, "No one was ever hurt, no life was ever lost on *Anne Kristine*. . . . For that we are, and forever will be, profoundly grateful." In his letter to Jen, Norman acknowledged:

> The loss depended on a whole string of events . . . [including] the timing of the hurricane: one day earlier and you would not have been caught; one day later and you would have been beyond range of rescue and at least some of you would be dead. Perhaps God thought, as payment for some of my earlier blunders from which I was saved, I owed Him a ship. But I didn't owe Him your lives. I just don't know.

After the reunion at the Bakers', I went home to Brooklyn and tried to resume life as I had known it. I went back to graveyards at the law firm, alternately enjoying and enduring the attention I got from my friends. I told the story again and again, as often as anyone wanted to hear it. Some of my friends heard it so often they started correcting me when I got something wrong. Other than that, I didn't think much about *Anne Kristine*. Then, in January 1992, I received a letter from Norman and Mary Ann, a letter they sent to the entire crew. It read: "We . . . started getting condolences from people who had heard *Anne Kristine* had come apart in severe weather, that planks had split, pumps had 'crapped out' and that she'd been abandoned for reasons of unseaworthiness."

This was news to me. Before this experience, I'd had no connection to the Bakers or the ship. I wasn't part of the sailing community. Apparently, this was big news in those circles, and as the Bakers wrote, the story "seemed to be spreading fast and far and wide. Norm heard it from fellow-members of the Explorers Club. Mary Ann heard it among friends here in the Berkshires. Our daughter Elizabeth heard it from friends in Boston." The rumors about *Anne Kristine* added another layer to the Bakers' heartbreak as well as the odd whiff of betrayal, because it was clear some of what was making the rounds could only have come from members of the crew.

The Bakers felt compelled to respond.

Significantly, the ship's log—the most accurate record of what we did and what decisions were made—was lost. When I talked with crew members in researching this book, no one could tell me what happened to it. But the log never made it back to the Bakers. So, Norman relied on the accounts of some crew members, the Coast Guard, and the log from *Ernestina*, the schooner that was also headed for Bermuda and sailed a similar route—up to a point.

In their letter to the crew, the Bakers acknowledged that "everyone aboard tried to the outer limits of their strength and endurance and ability to save her." But that was not enough. "In the end," they asserted, "it was a lack of familiarity with her systems that was her undoing." From conversations with Joey and other crew members, it became clear to Norman and Mary Ann that we made some basic errors that ultimately sealed the ship's fate.

For one thing, while we deployed oil bags, we didn't do so properly. Oil bags have been used for centuries by sailing ships to calm stormy waters. To work effectively, the canvas bag must be filled with a light-grade oil, then punctured repeatedly to ensure that the oil seeps out as it drags alongside the ship. The oil coats the water around the vessel so that the wind and the water lack the friction necessary to build a wave. Fish oil is considered the best oil to use in an oil bag; vegetable oil is number two. *Anne Kristine* always carried at least five gallons of vegetable oil. In normal circumstances, it was used for cooking, but there was plenty for the oil bags if the need arose. For some reason—because of lack of knowledge, the heat of the moment, or both—we used discarded engine oil, the worst option. And we never punctured the bags. The oil bags were in the water, but they weren't calming any waves.

We forgot to close all the vents on the ship's deck, and water came in that way. We didn't rig drogues. A drogue is a cone-shaped device made from fabric that drags behind the ship to help slow it down and prevent it from turning sideways into the waves. Instead we used the engine to control our speed, which not only put a strain on the engine but also kept us from using the engine's high-volume pump to keep the bilge from filling.

The Bakers wrote,

> You all tried sincerely, supremely hard to save her. But she didn't let you down either. And to hear from all around that she did fail you left us hurt and angered. Her pumps didn't crap out, and planks in place don't have room to split. When they fail, they rip loose their fastenings, and at 12 knots, the whole plank tears off. If *Anne Kristine* had popped a plank, you would not have had the time to be rescued, you would

have gone overboard in life rafts in minutes and many or
all of you might not have been here to read this.

Their words left me stunned. I liked the Bakers, and it seemed
unfair that they should be subjected to more pain than they had
already endured. It was like losing a child and then hearing rumors
questioning her character. They were forced to respond in the midst of
their mourning. Besides, I could not imagine which of the crew were
saying these things. In my narrative, there was no fault, only heroes:
we had fought heroically; *Anne Kristine* had cared for us heroically;
the Coast Guard crew had rescued us heroically. We had simply wandered into a storm that no one had predicted and that was larger than
anyone could have imagined.

Reality, of course, is never so simple, and neither are people. The
Bakers were hurt by the suggestion that their ship was less than sound.
Some of the crew were upset at the idea that we were responsible for
the loss of the ship, or that we had not done all we could to save her.
Almost thirty years later, I would finally sit down with most of the crew
and hear each person's memories and perspectives. For the first time
I heard their doubts about the ship and assertions of what happened.
And while I think they were sincere, I also think they were mistaken.

Back in Brooklyn, I did the only thing I knew to do. I kept talking, telling the story to anyone who would listen. That was my way of
understanding what I had been through, but each of us dealt with it in
our own way. Joey went home to South Carolina, where reporters had
already talked to his father and wanted to talk to him. "But I didn't
want to share it," he said. "I didn't want to glorify it." His great regret
was that "I didn't return a man's ship to him. But I feel that I did the
best that I could do. . . . I did my job, and every one of us made it."

Stuck between his mother, who told him it was OK to cry, and his
father, who told him to go out and get a real job, Joey tried to find a
way forward. He looked at his high school friends, who had settled

down, gotten married, raised kids. "And I was living out of a duffel bag at my mom's house," he told me. He decided to fulfill a lifelong dream. He would buy a farm.

To do that, he needed to save some money. After working as a roofer for several months, Joey got in his Plymouth Valiant and drove out to the Pacific Northwest, the place where he had first seen the Pacific Ocean. This time he had a five-hundred-ton license with a sailing addendum, and he had experience. He signed on to a fishing boat headed for Alaska. Did he feel any hesitation? "I went from a hurricane to fishing in the Bering Sea and forty-foot seas and seventy-mile-an-hour winds and breaking ice," he said. "People die up there. They get their hands cut. You go up there to make money."

Joey made money, enough to buy the two-hundred-year-old farm where he lives today.

In talking with my fellow crew members, I was struck by how most of them dealt with our experience, especially Damion and Peter, who told me they had not felt afraid at the time.

After the reunion at the Bakers', Damion was eager to get back on the water, so after a couple of weeks in South Carolina with Joey and a stint skiing in Colorado, he signed on to another tall ship in the spring of 1992, sailing the Atlantic for a year or two. "Winds took me west," he said, "where I got my captain's license." He worked seasonally, summers in Alaska and winters anywhere warm.

It was in Sitka, Alaska, that the past caught up with him. In the year 2000, Damion was working on a boat, taking high-dollar tourists out on eco-tours. He went to see *The Perfect Storm*, the movie with George Clooney as the captain of the doomed fishing boat *Andrea Gail*. The film's computer-generated effects were more than Damion could handle. "The monster wall of water and the windows blowing and all that stuff. That was hard on me, man," Damion remembered. "The mortality of it hit me. I went through a little PTSD. I had to leave the theater and I got in a bunch of trouble." He would not tell me what kind of trouble, but it landed him in the local jail.

Eventually, Damion also got tired of living out of a duffel bag. He moved back to Hawaii and started a nonprofit working with at-risk youth, using Hawaiian canoe paddling and sailing as educational tools. He studied, earned a bachelor's degree in anthropology and a master's degree in archaeology from the University of Hawaii. When I found him, he was a PhD candidate at the University of Oregon.

The surfer dude had discovered his inner academic. Damion planned to return to Hawaii after finishing his degree to continue working with young people.

Peter went sailing with a friend just a few days after the rescue, but he was subdued. His friend joked with him, asking Peter if he would feel better if the friend went below and put a hole in the bottom of the boat. When I asked him if he might have been in shock, Peter answered, "No, I don't think so." Then he told me:

> My daughter adored Norman and Mary Ann. They kind of adopted her. I was a single parent. My wife had died long, long ago. My daughter had made a couple of voyages [on *Anne Kristine*], one up to Nova Scotia. And she talked to me about coming on the trip to Bermuda. I knew Norman wasn't coming and I somehow convinced her that it wasn't a good idea.

"Why did you feel that way?" I asked.

"I don't know for sure."

What is certain is that his friendship with the Bakers—and his involvement with *Anne Kristine*—changed Peter's life. Their dream of circling the globe became his. When we left for Bermuda, Peter had begun studying to get his captain's license. After the rescue, he stopped. He just didn't see the point.

Some months later I received an invitation from Sikorsky Aircraft, the company that made the HH-60 helicopter. They had arranged a reunion with our rescuers. On a crisp, bright morning in early 1992, I took a train to Stratford, Connecticut, then a car service to Sikorsky company headquarters, where I found Barbara and Laingdon waiting. It was good to see them, though I was sorry to see we were the only three who had come. We were led down a long corridor to an exhibition room, where Paul Lange, David Morgan, John Julian, and Duane Jones were waiting. They looked impossibly dashing in their blue slacks and shimmering silver-gray flight jackets. And while we knew Sikorsky had set up the meeting as a photo op, I felt moved as I took each man's hand and thanked him. Later I learned that this was a rarity for them as well. Coast Guard crews almost never again see the people they have rescued. They were beaming.

Paul Lange was awarded the Distinguished Flying Cross for his heroism and skill on that night. The crew won an international award for rescue of the year. Years later I sat down with Lange, by then a retired Coast Guard commander, and asked him how that operation compared to the countless others he conducted over his long career. "Nothing compares to it," he said, "by a candle. And I made a lot of rescues. I probably saved 250 people that were actually dying. I hoisted thousands. Nothing comes close."

For Lange, a religious man, it was impossible not to see the hand of God in it. He felt it on the way home that night. No one could fly as well as he had without help. "No one can fly fifteen feet above fifty-foot waves and not get wet," he told me. "Nobody can fly out into a storm like this with a perfect complement of crew. It couldn't have been the luck of the draw. . . . Jesus still walks on the water, but you have to be drowning to see him. That's what I believed."

Lange's faith could not prepare him for the days after the rescue. He had nightmares, visions of flying into the water, of putting the tail of the helicopter into a rising wave. Of losing people. Five days after the rescue he ran in the Marine Corps Marathon, a race he had been training months to do. It did not go well. He felt "mamucked up" at mile 16 and barely finished. His wife Lib insisted he get checked out. He remembered, "We went to Portsmouth Naval Hospital and they said you've got a really low white blood cell count, and you need to prepare for your flying days to be over." Lange nodded, left the doctor's office, found the nearest trash can, and threw his medical report away. Shocked, Lib asked what he was doing. He answered that a lot of things were going to happen, "but quitting flying is not one of them." Soon after, Lange was transferred to Alaska, one of the Coast Guard's most challenging fields of operation. The nightmares subsided, his health improved, and he kept on flying.

Barbara and Laingdon kept in touch with me for a while after the Sikorsky visit. Laingdon and I shared the bond of being outsiders, the last two brought on board because the Bakers needed hands. I identified with his struggles on the ship, with the seasickness that debilitated him and with his courage in not giving in to it. Our time on the pump sealed our friendship. Barbara and I saw each other again at a lecture Norman gave about the family's *Anne Kristine* saga. I felt drawn to Barbara because of the experience we shared but realized that I knew nothing else about her. We saw each other a few times until her departure on another tall ship put her back at sea for several months. We lost touch after that.

Laingdon wrestled with his own demons in the aftermath. At one point he was living in a beach house in Connecticut, "and I realized that I was afraid to go down to the shore if it was windy at night." He began a gradual process of overcoming his fears. Each night he would walk toward the beach until the moment he felt the fear rising but before it overwhelmed him. He would stop and sit with it. The next night he would go a little farther.

Laingdon kept sailing. His last professional tall ship job was the summer of '95 in the St. Lawrence Seaway and Canadian Maritimes.

Always drawn to creative endeavors, he took a degree in fine arts in 1998, moved out West a year later, and settled in Port Townsend, Washington, for a time. While there he helped raise a couple of kids. When I tracked him down, he was living in central Oregon, where he worked as a handyman and contractor. In 2020 he wrote to me, "No more boats (sold my last boat a month ago, up in Port Townsend), just rock climbing and motorcycles now."

Our experience had a profound effect on Barbara that stayed with her ever after. "Taking the step off the boat in darkness into the unknown has given me a sense of faith beyond any religion," she told me, "of the unknowing we all experience." She too sailed again, taking a last-minute offer as cook on the *Rose*, a three-masted frigate, for Op Sail '92, the quincentennial commemoration of Columbus's landing in America. Barbara stayed on the *Rose* for three months, finally making it to Bermuda that summer. "I do not fear the sea," she wrote me, though that was her last time on the water. She moved to Chapel Hill, North Carolina, where she lives with her partner and their son. "I teach yoga and live very much in the present moment as my experiences have taught me," she said. "Every day is an adventure."

The two crew members I was not able to interview for this book were Marty Hanks and Jen Irving. I found Jen, but she declined to talk with me. "That's your story," she said. I do know that the experience left her badly shaken, and that she and Norman wrote to each other about it in the months afterward. She continued working as a professional sailor, including a time as a ship's captain for the National Oceanic and Atmospheric Administration. She now lives quietly, still surrounded by water, on Cape Cod, Massachusetts.

I never found Marty, though it was not for lack of trying. I searched for him many times and in many ways. I called a lot of wrong numbers in Hawaii, where I believe he moved with his family after the rescue. If you're reading this, Marty, I hope the years have treated you kindly, and that I got it mostly right.

When I asked crew members to summarize their lives since our voyage, no one did it any better than John Nuciforo. His account reads like an outsize haiku of a life well lived:

> Thirty years in a few words? OK, let's go. After Hurricane Grace sinks plans of sailing the Caribbean, a fresh start. Colorado! Move to the mountains, work for Vail Associates, ski brains out at Beaver Creek. Hitchhike north to Alaska. Slime salmon, hide from bears, and sleep under the stars. Study Spanish in Guatemala, travel through Central and South America, scuba dive Galapagos. Lose parents, a setback. Home in the beautiful Berkshires. Drive big rigs. Back to school, earn [Massachusetts] Teacher's License, teach at a small public school. Present planetarium shows and go on solar eclipse expeditions with Williams College. Move to Arizona with my girlfriend to be closer to her father. Sonoran Desert sweat, dreams of world travel persist. Lots of ins and outs, look forward to the future. Thank you, US Coast Guard.

Yes, thank you, US Coast Guard.

10

CODA

———

FOR MARY ANN, people were always what mattered most. Perhaps that's why of all the Bakers, she seemed best able to move on from the loss of *Anne Kristine*. Their beloved schooner was gone, but the nine of us were still here, and that seemed to even the scales somehow.

In the years that followed, Mary Ann continued to be the beating heart of her clan and her community, embracing Norman through his darkest times, fussing after her children and newly arriving grandchildren, tending to her many friendships. She placed herself at the center of life in Berkshire County. She taught reading to adults. She worked with youngsters at St. Agnes' School in Dalton. She became chairwoman of Windsor's Open Space Plan, helped found the Windsor Land Trust, and was an active member of the Arts Council of Windsor. Mary Ann brought to all of it the same joy, love, and stick-to-itiveness that had seen her through the hardest days of the rebuild.

At age sixty, she enrolled in a writing workshop and began writing stories and poems that appeared in several anthologies, and later worked as an investigative journalist for *The Women's Times*, an award-winning regional publication.

In 1997 I ran into Mary Ann, Norman, and Mitchell while on the Boston-New York AIDS Ride. The Bakers' youngest child had contracted HIV in the early '90s, and participating in the four-day, three-hundred-mile cycling fundraiser was their show of support. With thousands of cyclists and volunteers dotting the route, finding the three of them at a rest stop somewhere in the middle of Connecticut seemed like providence itself. We sat together and ate the boxed lunch provided to us, talked about the ride, and caught up. I had not seen the Bakers in several years, and this chance meeting rekindled our acquaintance and my desire to tell our story. Soon after I asked Norman if he would sit down with me for an in-depth interview. The following year I traveled to their home in western Massachusetts. It was the last time I saw Mary Ann.

In late July 2001, "my nonsmoking, yoga-doing, healthy-eating mother got lung cancer," Mitchell told me. She died in 2003 at the age of sixty-six, much, much too soon.

―――――――――

Never a man to give up easily on anything that mattered, Norman tried for several years to raise the money to build *Anne Kristine II*. He finished the documentary, wrote a book about the experience, lectured. As had happened in Tortola, he was the only person who did not know it couldn't be done. The difference was that this time he was wrong, and the naysayers were right. Rebuilding a gutted hundred-year-old schooner with his family was one thing; building that same schooner from scratch was an endeavor of a different magnitude. In a life in which he had defied the odds time and again, this was one quixotic dream too far.

After Mary Ann's death Norman moved in with Elizabeth and her family, where he got to enjoy the role of coolest grandpa ever while not slowing down at all. He continued to travel the world as explorer, adventurer, and lecturer with fellow explorers and adventurers old and new. He was revered wherever he went.

He also continued to fly. His 1966 Cessna was the one place, at age eighty-nine, that he felt unimpaired, where he could still be that seventeen-year-old boy and "slip the surly bonds of earth." The afternoon before Thanksgiving 2017 he took off from Pittsfield Municipal Airport. It was Daniel's turn to host at his home in Vermont, and Norman was excited to spend the holiday with his family. When he did not arrive, they called the police. They found the wreckage of his Cessna 172G, which he had named *Anne Kristine II*, in some woods ten miles south of Middlebury.

An investigation by the National Transportation Safety Board found that both pilot and plane were sound. It was raining, and some fog had formed. The cloud ceiling was two thousand feet, as it had been all those years before, when he had barely survived his first bad scrape with the skies. Then he had been lucky. This time it seems he became disoriented in the worsening weather. He had likely been using Route 7 as a guide to steer by and veered north, into a narrow valley where he was hemmed in by ridges to both sides and the low clouds above. He tried to get back over Route 7. He turned east to avoid one hill, then swung sharply west. Flying barely 425 feet above the ground, Norman managed to clear a hidden lake and another ridge. When he struck a tree, Route 7 was just a few hundred feet away.

I learned of Norman's death from a friend's e-mail that started, "You've probably heard by now . . . " I hadn't, as I was just returning from Thanksgiving with my own family. I sat for a long time, stunned. It was shocking news, yet somehow not surprising. Something drove Norman Baker his entire life, pushed him toward the edge, forced him to look down into the darkness below to see . . . what? I sat looking out the window as night fell, knowing it could not have ended any other way.

———————

Over the years people have asked me again and again, "How did it change you?" And I always detect in their voice the hope that it changed everything. Indeed, how could anyone live through something like this without being affected in some profound way? And the truth is that it did. And it didn't. I didn't come back and alter my life in some radical way. I went back to the graveyard shift, for a while at least. I continued to live what to all outward appearances was a fairly conventional life.

But one thing occurs to me: standing on the deck that night, staring up at the light, stunned and scared and wondering how I'd gotten there, wondering if I would survive, I felt completely alive. And the challenge has been to realize that I was no more alive then than I am now, as I write this, or when I'm walking in the park, enjoying the sun, or when I'm sitting in my room, feeling bored. I am never any more or less alive at any moment than I am at any other, if I but choose to notice. A hurricane helps you notice. A hurricane will get your attention. But it's not, strictly speaking, necessary.

Another thing I learned is that once you have survived something like this, you are considered something of a good-luck charm among sailing people, and they want you along. I got lots of invitations. Two years later, I sailed on another tall ship, this one out of Boston. Laingdon was aboard as well. We sailed to Martha's Vineyard. We sailed those waters for several days. And . . . Nothing. Bad. Happened.

EPILOGUE

QUESTIONS

———

"Everyone made it back ashore safely. That is worth noting!"
—Gregg Swanzey, captain of *Ernestina*

TWO THINGS ARE CERTAIN about the last voyage of *Anne Kristine*: the ship was lost, and all nine crew members survived. Beyond that, we are left with many questions that were raised at the time yet remain unanswered thirty years on. Did we plot the best course? Did the pumps work properly? Did we make mistakes that worsened our plight? Different versions of what happened emerged at the time, even among the crew members themselves. Broadly speaking, they come down to two narratives. In the first, we did things right (or at least mostly right), and *Anne Kristine* let us down—"planks had split, pumps had 'crapped out,' and she'd been abandoned for reasons of unseaworthiness," according to the rumors the Bakers heard. In the other version, the fault lay not with the ship but with ourselves, our "human frailty," Norman called it, "and we all have our share."

The story I have told in this book is my best reckoning of what occurred on that journey, what we did, and the decisions we made. As the ninth crew member and admitted "accidental sailor," my memories of our experience are more sensory than informational. I remember vividly huddling in a growing pool of water as Laingdon and I pumped the tiny head pump for hours. I don't remember—nor did I know at the time—what course we plotted or when. I was overpowered by the fumes of the gasoline we poured below deck to refill the deck pump. I did not understand why that pump became our last failing lifeline in the hours before our rescue. I did what was asked of me and avoided asking for explanations.

To understand our story as fully as possible, I spoke with as many of the other crew members as I could track down—six in all—to hear and compare their memories of our experience. I spoke at length with Paul Lange, though I never found any of his crew. I talked with Pete Stein, the C-130 pilot who was on the air base radio that night and managed to locate the aircraft carrier where Lange refueled. I interviewed Mitchell, Elizabeth, and Dan Baker. For perspective and expertise, I spoke with two experienced tall ship captains, one of whom commanded *Ernestina* through the same storm. Most important, I went back to interviews I conducted not long after the experience, when memories were fresher and more reliable. One, a talk I had with Peter Abelman, occurred just two months after the rescue. In 1998 I traveled to the Bakers' home in western Massachusetts and taped a six-hour conversation with Norman over two days.

Two of the most important records were the ship's log and the Coast Guard files associated with the *Anne Kristine* case. The log is a ship's official record. In it is recorded every significant decision and course change, including comments that would offer insight into what the captain was thinking and how the crew were doing. The captain is responsible for the log, and Joey vaguely remembered taking it with him, but it is not clear what happened to it after the rescue. It never got to the Bakers.

The Coast Guard case files contained the official records of the rescue, including the reports filed by the crews of the rescue helicopter and the C-130 plane that attempted to drop us pumps, and the air base radio operators. Paul Lange told me there was no record of the communication between him and the ship, but that communications originating from the Coast Guard base would have been recorded. From these I wanted to assemble a narrative of our final hours from the perspective of the rescuers. When did we first contact the Coast Guard? What information did we tell them about our position and condition? What were the exact coordinates of our rescue?

I began searching for those records shortly after I located Paul Lange in spring 2019. After more than a year of searching—including three Freedom of Information Act requests, countless unanswered phone calls and unreturned messages, months of bouncing around the Coast Guard bureaucracy, and then everything grinding to a halt when the COVID-19 pandemic struck the United States—I finally learned the bad news: Unless a case is "historically significant" (involves a prominent politician, say, or some other public figure), Coast Guard case files are kept for only a limited number of years. Then they are destroyed.

The *Anne Kristine* case files were long gone.

───────────

When the Bakers first heard that a storm was building south of Bermuda, they were concerned. "After all, that was our ship out there," said Norman. "There was a hurricane out there. But I kept telling Mary Ann that with the sailing speed of *Anne Kristine* there's no reason why she would not have headed west immediately with a hurricane south of her." As they tracked Grace's progress and estimated our position, they figured we were running west, possibly to tuck in at

Cape May along the southern tip of the New Jersey shore, or perhaps as far south as the Chesapeake Bay.

But we did not turn west when we first heard about Tropical Storm Grace. Peter Abelman, who was helping chart our course, told me two months after the rescue that we adjusted our course slightly east to try to skirt around the storm. In 1998 Norman asserted the same thing based on his conversations with both Peter and Joey immediately after the rescue.

In their ship's log, the crew of *Ernestina* noted that they heard the Coast Guard's response to our distress call at 6:00 PM on October 28, several hours before our rescue. They wrote that we were "100 miles to windward [or northeast] of us. Our position is 35° 50'Nx72° 40'W." That was our last approximate position on record. *Ernestina*'s coordinates placed them about two hundred miles off the coast of North Carolina, and *Anne Kristine* an additional one hundred miles at sea. If we had turned west at the first sign of trouble, would we have ended up that far off the coast at the time of our rescue? And wouldn't our course have been much more like *Ernestina*'s, which avoided the worst of the storm?

Captain Jan Miles is a tall-ship master with more than fifty years' experience as a professional sailor. Whenever I reached out to him for an expert's perspective, he always responded with a nuanced, layered analysis of each issue I presented. In this case he used all the information he could gather to reconstruct conditions and imagine our likely route. He studied *Ernestina*'s log, including their depiction of the Gulf Stream. He plotted the distance and direction of the helicopter as described in newspaper articles written at the time. He plotted what he could of *Anne Kristine*'s movements as described by me and several articles, including the estimate written in *Ernestina*'s log.

He plotted Grace's movements, as well as tropical-storm-force winds (those greater than thirty-nine miles per hour) extending to the northwest of the storm center. To gain insight into Grace's behavior, Miles studied a federal government report on the Perfect Storm that included all of Grace's movements, as well as a depiction of conditions leading up to the stronger storm that occurred later and farther to the northeast. In this report he referred to the surface analysis map, a depiction of air pressure at the ocean's surface in the storm. By cross-referencing the surface analysis map with the log of *Ernestina* in the days leading up to the rescue, Miles could form an impression of surface winds and the overall sea conditions during our final hours.

Miles concluded that *Anne Kristine* did not turn west for some time after Grace had become a significant disturbance but continued on a southeast trajectory "up till turning downwind/down-sea toward the west because of wind strength making up a bigger sea from the east and eventually the northeast." He also seemed skeptical of *Ernestina*'s estimate of our location at the time of our distress call to the Coast Guard at 6:00 PM on the twenty-eighth, and by extrapolation the precise location of our rescue.

Given his calculations of our position in the storm and *Ernestina*'s coordinates per their log, Miles concluded that the weather conditions we experienced were comparable to those confronted by the other schooner. This is a debatable point. *Ernestina* certainly sailed through rough seas. Their log indicates "frequent boarding by 25-30' seas" and a "Force 9 wind." Force 9 on the Beaufort scale means severe gale-force winds, likely over fifty miles per hour. By the time *Ernestina* weathered those conditions, they were well west of the storm and *Anne Kristine* and had begun sailing south, parallel to the coast of North Carolina. By our own reckoning and other accounts, we endured hurricane-force winds of seventy-five miles per hour and above during the worst of our ordeal. Still, it is certainly possible that by the time of our distress call in the twilight of the twenty-eighth, when *Ernestina* captured the Coast Guard's response, we were sailing in conditions like theirs. By then, of course, we were in much worse shape.

That brings us to the condition of the ship and the functioning of the pumps. When all other factors are considered, the key differences that decided the fates of *Ernestina* and *Anne Kristine* seem to be each ship's ability to keep water from coming aboard and capacity to remove the water that did. The crew of *Ernestina*—all thirty-five of them—were never overwhelmed by the conditions they encountered. They lashed all boxes and gear and battened down hatches early, on October 26, just as we were setting out. With plenty of experienced hands on board, as well as trainees, *Ernestina*'s crew battled the elements, but they were never forced to battle their own fatigue.

By contrast, our small, patchwork crew was pushed to the edge early and forced to stay there until the moment of our rescue. As a result, we missed things. In his letter to Jen, Norman expressed surprise that she remembered to stuff the chain pipes, which prevented water from entering *Anne Kristine* through those openings. He told her, "What you did could not have been done better," and went on to say, "I know you were all working on overload at the time, and it's understandable that the chain pipe closings didn't trigger remembrance of the galley and engine room vents." Water came in through those openings and poured below deck.

Did water come in from below? It's possible that some did. "Old ships leak" is a truism I heard more than once in researching tall ships. Gregg Swanzey, the captain of *Ernestina*, told me about a barkentine he worked on that did Arctic exploration near Greenland and humpback whale studies in the Caribbean. "Notorious for leaking," he said. "Oh my God." How did they deal with it? "You just have to have pumps that keep up with it," he said.

A ship in a storm is being "worked." In sailing terms this means the hull is being twisted, bent, and pushed by the phenomenal forces generated by a hurricane. A wooden ship can withstand these conditions because wood is flexible. It will bend and give. The question is, How much can a vessel give before it breaks? As near as I can tell from my recollections and from the experts I have spoken to, *Anne Kristine* never reached this breaking point. There were moments where she seemed pushed to the limit, where the creaks of wood being worked turned to howls that made me wonder how much more the ship could take. But in the end, *Anne Kristine* held. As the Bakers asserted in their letter to us, and others have since supported, in those conditions planks don't come apart a little bit. If planks had torn loose, the ship would have filled quickly, and I probably would not be here to tell about it.

Some of our crew thought they saw oakum in the detritus floating in the bilge. They pointed to this as evidence that the ship's caulking was being worked out of the seams and causing the ship to leak. And they said that this material was clogging the pumps, making it impossible for the pumps to work properly. Oakum is a loosely twisted ropelike material made from oiled jute or hemp fibers. It has been used to seal hull seams from the earliest days of shipbuilding and is so effective that its use has changed little since. Oakum was originally made from old tarry ropes that were unraveled by hand and reduced to fiber, a process called "picking." It was important work, but so tedious and painful that it was done by inmates in prisons and workhouses.

Three expert sources—including both Captains Miles and Swanzey—told me that if any oakum had been worked loose, it would not have ended up inside the ship. It would have gone out rather than in. There may have been junk in the bilge as it filled with water, but it wasn't oakum.

Which brings us to the pumps. When Joey put out a distress call around 6:00 PM on the twenty-eighth, it was clear that we were not keeping up. Wherever the water was coming from, *Anne Kristine* was filling. The Coast Guard tried three times to drop us a pump and failed each time. By the time we were rescued, Hurricane Grace had finally turned east, and we were no longer being pummeled. The worst, it seemed, was over, and the ship was still sailing. When I asked

Paul Lange his impression of how low in the water the schooner was when he first found us, he said it was hard to tell because he didn't know what was normal for this particular vessel. Water was washing across the deck, but not enough to knock people off their feet. When we jumped, we "were falling a bit to hit the water," he remembered. "It wasn't like people were just stepping into the seas." He noticed the sails were "tore to pieces, and she was literally making eight or nine knots just on bare sticks, literally surfing down waves." Lange was surprised that the ship was still so buoyant. "You can't do that if you're underwater," he told me.

Aboard *Anne Kristine* several of the crew debated until the moment of their rescue whether they might still sail the ship home. However high their emotions, they must have thought they had a real chance of saving her; they weren't devoid of judgment.

In his analysis of our situation, Captain Miles concluded that "the only thing that caused the need . . . to abandon *Anne Kristine*" was that we were "having problems evacuating the water that was accumulating aboard and inside [the ship]."

In other words, if the pumps had been pumping properly, we could have sailed *Anne Kristine* to safety. What happened? Of all the failures that led to the loss of the schooner, this one seems the most contentious, the hardest for me to grasp, and the one most steeped with regret. When Norman took Joey below deck to go over the pumps with him before our departure, Peter Abelman wanted to join them. He had been sailing with the Bakers for several years and had never operated the pumps, and this seemed like a good time to learn. Norman waved him off, saying that he had more important things for him to do at that moment. Thirty years later, Peter still regretted not insisting. As a result, Joey was the only person on board who knew how to work the various pumps, some of which were tricky to operate even in calm conditions. What was it like in the middle of a hurricane, with no one to help him and so much else to keep track of?

According to Joey, the various pumps were working properly at first, sucking large quantities of water from the ship. The problems commenced when they began to clog with oakum (if, indeed, there was oakum present) and other debris floating in the bilge. When that happened, he would turn off the pump, unclog it, and turn it back on. Or else a pump would begin to overheat and would be turned off until it cooled down. This went on for hours as one pump would run, then go out, then come back. Then another. In his recollection, the pumps kept us afloat for a long time, but eventually they were no longer able to keep up with the water coming on board.

Norman told a different story based on his conversations with Joey, Peter, and other crew members. When I spoke with him in 1998, Norman recounted in detail the process of demonstrating the operation of the centrifugal pumps to the young captain shortly before we left Brooklyn. He opened the sea cock to flood the ship, then opened the priming valves. It took several minutes for the water to completely cover the pump's impellers. Only then did Norman turn on the pump, and it quickly emptied the water from the bilge.

Norman was convinced that Joey had not primed the pumps properly. "I asked," said Norman, "'Did you check to see that the pumps were pumping?'

'Yeah, I looked over the side.'

'Was water coming out?'

'Yeah, a little.'

'What do you mean, "a little"? If that pump worked, it would have shot a bolt of water out of the ship three inches in diameter. And it would have gone out of the ship twenty feet before it fell into the sea.'"

Norman told me, "Those pumps were full of air and never sucked a teaspoon of water out of that ship. They only pumped out the priming water itself."

Besides the large centrifugal pumps *Anne Kristine* had another high-volume option in its arsenal of pumps. Normally, the ship's engine drew its cooling water from the sea. But before the voyage, the Bakers had installed a valve to switch the suction to a hose from the bilge. This would allow the engine to cool itself while drawing water from the bilge with what Norman called "the most effective, highest volume pump on the entire ship." When I asked Joey about it, he told me that he was using this pump, and it was working successfully. But that was not Norman's impression. He said that Joey told him he avoided using the main engine pump for fear it would overheat because of the debris being sucked up from the bilge. This would have been a catastrophic failure. We needed the engine to keep us from broaching as we were being swept down the faces of the waves. Whenever we felt the ship turning, we kicked in the engine and used the rudder to keep us facing exactly downwind. If we had broached, we would have capsized. Norman's answer was that the hose was outfitted with a screen to prevent clogging, and additional, finer mesh screens were kept in the engine room.

None of the rest of the crew had a clear recollection of how well or poorly the pumps were working. It seems no one was by Joey's side as he tried to troubleshoot the problems that arose. And, besides, we were all stretched to our limits, trying simply to keep up with the tasks at hand, whether that meant steering the ship, working the gasoline or hand pumps, operating the radio, or simply providing hot broth to keep everyone going. When I asked, each crew member had an *impression* of how the pumps were working. Some seemed to agree with Joey's assertion that oakum (or some other debris) was clogging the hoses and keeping the pumps from pumping to capacity. Others had the sense that the pumps were not used properly from the beginning.

To get some insight and outside perspective, I sent Captains Swanzey and Miles both Norman's and Joey's account to see what they made of them. Miles found Norman's discussion of priming mostly consistent and logical. Centrifugal pumps are not self-priming, he said. And when they work properly, they throw a lot of water. We would have seen a powerful jet stream of water coming off the ship.

Swanzey, who captained *Ernestina* through the same storm, acknowledged that it could be difficult to know exactly where the failure lay: with the pumps, the way we used them, or a combination of the two. "Priming pumps can be tricky," he wrote, "and some types of pumps are more challenging than others. [C]logged strainers at the intakes for the pumps are also likely when the ship is rolling, and it is easy to have objects go into the bilge. It takes constant vigilance." Perhaps thinking about *Ernestina*'s own experienced crew and its mission as a training vessel, Swanzey wondered about our lack of familiarity and training to handle such a situation. "Were there drills?" he asked. "Obviously, the captain was attempting to get the pumps going, but was there an engineer or other crew that also had the knowledge? The captain has plenty else to deal with."

Swanzey also wondered about the handling of the ship. When he told me about *Ernestina*'s journey, I was surprised to hear that they had weathered the entire storm under sail, mostly trysails—small, strong sails designed to be used in heavy winds. A trysail provides enough thrust to maintain control of the ship while tempering the vessel's speed. They didn't use their engine through most of the storm; in fact, *Ernestina*'s engine was flooded by salt water, and Swanzey and crew didn't even notice until October 30, after they had left the worst of the storm behind. A sailing ship is built to *sail*, the captain told me. The challenge was to use the right sail combinations and balance so that the ship could naturally orient itself to the wind and move at a manageable speed. He wrote, "If a balance is struck, the rolling [of the ship] is diminished and there is some control at the helm."

I don't think we had trysails on *Anne Kristine*. Instead, we kept shortening our sails over the course of the final two days. In the end we were left with bare sticks, headed dead downwind and trying to control the ship's stability and speed using only engine power.

Pointing out that every situation is different, Swanzey told me that conditions in a storm can vary even within short distances, and that it was not his place to criticize the decisions a fellow captain had to make in his hardest moments. He wrote,

> It is easy to sit in a warm room ashore and second guess those at sea. As you know, I have been one of those out there and have seen plenty of challenges that we came through but could have handled differently in retrospect. Everyone made it back ashore safely. That is worth noting!

———————

Another issue that has puzzled me over the years is that of the ship's insurance. Namely, *Anne Kristine* didn't have any. Or at least she wasn't insured against damage or loss. (I assume the Bakers had liability insurance to cover the injury or death of a crew member.) At the time my impression was that the schooner was insured for sailing in coastal waters, like its customary route between New York and Nova Scotia, but that this coverage ended the minute we entered "blue water." This concept seemed reasonable, and I didn't give it much thought. But once I did consider it, I could not let it go. If *Anne Kristine* had been insured, she could have been replaced, and the great tragedy of the Baker family inestimably reduced. On *Anne Kristine II*, the Caribbean plans could have been salvaged, and eventually, the dream of circumnavigation realized.

In researching this book, I asked both crew and family members what they remembered about the ship's insurance. One of the Bakers told me that its insurance policy was changing because the ship's tax status was transitioning from a nonprofit to a for-profit venture. The old policy expired at midnight on October 28; the new policy was scheduled to begin at noon on October 29. Since we lost the ship sometime after midnight, *Anne Kristine* was uninsured when she went down. When I asked an insurance agent who specializes in maritime policies, he replied, "The tax status doesn't come into play in policies we write. What the boat does (day sails, sail training, fishing) does matter, but not tax status."

No one else had a clear impression of why *Anne Kristine* would have set off without being fully covered. Insurance for a vessel that old would have been expensive. Is it possible Norman simply didn't have the money to insure the schooner and was counting on the funds from the Caribbean expeditions to pay for a policy going forward? It is the question that most haunts me, the one thing I would ask Norman if I could. Why, why, why would you allow *Anne Kristine*, your most prized possession, your fourth child, to leave dock without insurance? Insurance is protection against the unthinkable, and the unthinkable happened.

Finally, I am left wondering about the call that never came. Norman was convinced that he could have saved *Anne Kristine* if we had just called him. In their letter telling friends of the ship's loss, the Bakers wrote, "Norman, in the quiet of our home, would have told [the captain] what to do about so much that was overwhelming him in the storm, that was too much for a young man in extremis." In his letter to Jen, Norman notes, "You and Joey were at the radios for hours. The one thing I must ask is this: Why was I not called? I can think of several possible answers." He goes on to list eight reasons that might have prevented his captain and first mate from contacting him, from not thinking of it to being too embarrassed to feeling it would not have made a difference. While I understand Norman's frustration and agree that having the benefit of his analytical mind and experience would have helped, I am not surprised that the call was never made. We were slammed from the first crisis to the moment Joey was lifted from the sea. He and the other experienced crew were pulled a hundred different ways in keeping us afloat and moving toward safety. A call in those conditions seems a lot to expect.

Instead, what might have saved us was a practice that is routine on expeditions like ours. As Peter Abelman told me, "Norman should have insisted that we call him twice a day. There's no reason not to. And I have no idea in the world why Norman didn't do that. Would that have made a difference? I think so."

"Why?"

"We would not have turned east. We would not have turned north. We would have turned west."

Ernestina's Route

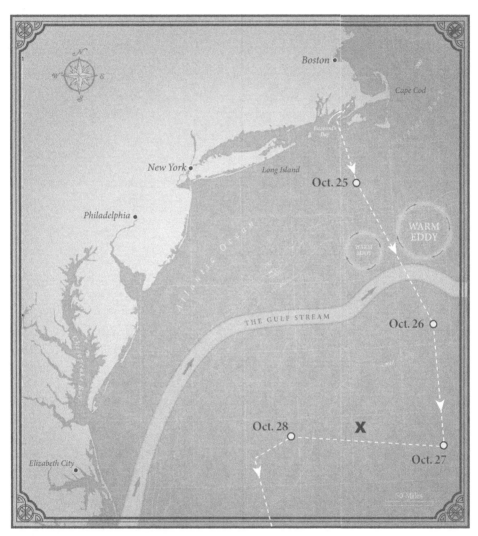

This map shows the route of the schooner *Ernestina* after it set sail from Cape Cod on October 25, en route to St. Georges, Bermuda. Each date shows the ship's position at noon. The *X* at the bottom right shows the approximate location of *Anne Kristine* around 6:00 PM on October 28, when *Ernestina* picked up the Coast Guard's radio response to our distress call.

ACKNOWLEDGMENTS

WRITING IS A SOLITARY ACT, but making a book takes lots of people, and help has come from many directions over many years. To everyone who told me I should "write a book" and those who finally made me sit down and do it, I thank you, and I'm sorry for doubting you. Let these pages stand as your resounding, collective "I told you so."

Thanks to the crew of *Anne Kristine* for keeping me alive, and to those of you who were kind enough to sit down with me and talk about our experience: Joey Gelband, Damion Sailors, Peter Abelman, Barbara Treyz, John Nuciforo, and Laingdon Schmitt. To the Baker family—Elizabeth Atwood, Mitchell Baker, and Dan Baker—thank you for sharing your memories of your parents and of *Anne Kristine*. It could not have been easy, but you were gracious and generous in equal measure. To Paul Lange, for bringing alive the rescue from your unique perspective, and to Pete Stein, for filling in an important part of the narrative.

For helping me understand and explore the nautical aspects of the story, I am grateful to Gregg Swanzey and Jan Miles, tall ship captains with over fifty years' collective experience at the helm. On the subject of hurricanes—their science and legend—I could not have done better than Dr. Kerry Emanuel of MIT. Ed Rappaport of the National Hurricane Center helped me understand the nuts and bolts of tracking hurricanes, in addition to the particular nature and idiosyncrasies of Hurricane Grace.

Before there was a book, there was "The Accidental Sailor," the storytelling performance on which it was based. My thanks to Maeve Gately and Robert Burke of Hudson River Community Sailing, who first invited me to be part of their speaker series, then invited me back a second time. Many thanks to everyone at the venues that followed: Libby Daly from Mystic Seaport Museum (Mystic, CT); Lee Gruzen from the New York Ship Lore and Model Club; Nomi Dayan and Liz Fusco from the Whaling Museum and Education Center at Cold Spring Harbor (Long Island, NY); Joan Lowenthal for the Northport Yacht Club and Centerport Yacht Club (Long Island, NY); Robert Pillsbury, Richard Rosenblatt, and Karen Loew from the Salmagundi Art Club (New York, NY); Lori Robishaw and Kelli Rocherole from La Grua Center (Stonington, CT); Linda Dianto and Tina Cuadrado from the National Lighthouse Museum (Staten Island, NY); Rina Kleege, Hollis Headrick, Rebecca Martinez, and Noel Hefele from PLGArts (Brooklyn, NY); Logan Irons from the Beach Point Club (Mamaroneck, NY); and Kathy VandeLaare and Barbara Walkowski from the Grosse Pointe Yacht Club (Detroit, MI).

To Antonio Rosario, for his beautiful video work. To Nagi Argiriou, who created the website that gave "The Accidental Sailor" its first home online. To Michael Evans, whose stunning, layered sound design brought the piece more to life than ever. To Susan Hefner, artist, mentor, and friend, with whom I have shared a life's worth of creativity and fun.

A special thanks to Virginia Depetris, who envisioned this book long before I did. Virginia engineered a presentation of "The

Accidental Sailor" at her local library for the express purpose of getting her friend the literary agent there. When the friend called at the last minute to cancel, Virginia told her to get in her car and drive, then held the curtain a full twenty minutes until her friend arrived.

To Stacey Glick, my literary agent, thanks for not staying home, and for guiding me with kindness, clarity, and grace from the start.

To Brendan Spiegel, the cofounder and editorial director at Narratively, the online storytelling platform that published an early version of my story that helped demonstrate a book was possible.

To Jerry Pohlen, Ben Krapohl, and all the folks at Chicago Review Press for giving me a chance to hold this book in my hands.

A big thanks to all my friends, old and new, who supported me through each step of the process: to Phoebe Law, whose curiosity made her the first person who *wasn't* already a friend to check out my presentation. To the Skadden gang, who were there from the beginning: Peter Honschaurk, Jonny Rosenblatt, Paul Maggio, Tim Wilson, and Nora Presutti, my little sister. To Linda Hardwick and Clara Lee (aka the Humbugs), who watched over me along the way. To Stella Varveris, loyal friend, honest critic, emergency contact. It was Stella who, during a particularly low moment in the writing, told me to get mad at the book. I did, and it helped.

Finally, to my parents, Nazira and Selim, and my siblings, Fatima and Roberto. Thank you always.